MADE TO ORDER: THE SHEETZ STORY

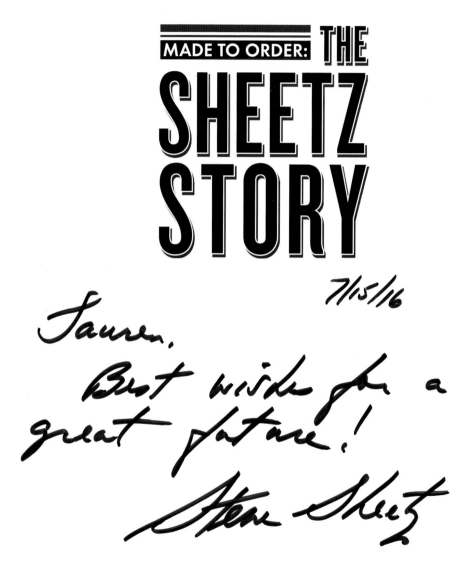

7/15/16

Lauren,
Best wishes for a
great future!

Steve Sheetz

The Fifth Avenue Dairy's horse and buggy are pictured here around 1910. (Courtesy of Sheetz.)

ON THE COVER: (Inset top) The first Sheetz Dairy Store under Bob Sheetz's ownership opened on November 1, 1952, at Fifth and Union Avenues in Altoona. The store was later renamed Sheetz Kwik Shopper. (Inset bottom) From left to right, Steve, Bob, and Stan Sheetz visit a Sheetz store. (Both courtesy of Sheetz.)

MADE TO ORDER: THE SHEETZ STORY

Kenneth Womack

ARCADIA
PUBLISHING

Published by Arcadia Publishing
Charleston, South Carolina

Printed in the United States of America

Library of Congress Control Number: 2013939116

For all general information, please contact Arcadia Publishing:
Telephone 843-853-2070
Fax 843-853-0044
E-mail sales@arcadiapublishing.com
For customer service and orders:
Toll-Free 1-888-313-2665

Visit us on the Internet at www.arcadiapublishing.com

For Joseph M. "Big Joe" Sheetz (1945–2006).

CONTENTS

FOREWORD

It is fitting that *Made to Order: The Sheetz Story* is dedicated to Joe Sheetz, who passed away in August 2006. In many ways, Joseph M. "Big Joe" Sheetz was our company's heart and soul, an abiding moral compass who helped mold Sheetz into the progressive, family-oriented organization that it is today. For more than 20 years, Big Joe served as the head of store development, a period in which the company enjoyed dynamic and unparalleled growth. But even more importantly, Big Joe was a beloved family man and a dedicated, active member of his community.

As we look back over the past six decades, we are proud of our company's many contributions to the shaping and reshaping of retail culture into the new century. But we are even more proud of the way in which we grew the organization, through the leadership and vision of Bob Sheetz, from a one-store operation in 1952 to more than 450 locations today. Through our collective efforts, we established a company that is unfailingly customer and employee oriented, that never shies away from doing the right thing, and, above all, places people and their welfare before anything else.

In his own right, Joe was a great champion of these ideals. Not surprisingly, Big Joe was instrumental in the creation of our For the Kidz charities. For the Kidz dates back to 1992, when district managers Dan McMahon and Charlie Campbell led the company's employee base in raising $12,000 to help out 126 disadvantaged children during the holidays. Since its humble beginnings, the initiative has raised $11.6 million to support more than 69,000 children. After his death in 2006, we honored Joe's character and passion for philanthropy through the Big Joe Scholarship Fund, which provides vital learning opportunities for the children and stepchildren of our employees based upon their academic success, overall excellence of character, community involvement, and leadership. We know, in our hearts, that these are the very characteristics that Joe valued above all else and—perhaps even more significantly—that he would have cherished the most in creating brighter futures for today's youth.

As we ponder our company's long history through the pages of this book, we cannot help thinking about all of the changes that have impacted our industry since the early 1950s. Back then, it was all but impossible to imagine the technological innovations and cultural shifts that have dramatically altered our business in countless ways. But through it all, our family has existed as a singular source of strength and continuity through such rapidly changing times. We pledge that Sheetz will continue to celebrate this strength by cementing itself as a family-oriented business. To this end, we are proud to note that Big Joe's son, Joe S. "Joey" Sheetz, assumed the mantle of leadership as our company's chief executive officer in October 2013. Through Joey's new role with Sheetz, we are both welcoming in a new generation of leadership and maintaining our company's legacy at the same time. As always, we are excited by the prospects to come as we write the next chapter of our company's history.

—Steve and Stan Sheetz

ACKNOWLEDGMENTS

This book would not have been possible without the efforts of Bob and Steve Sheetz, who gave generously of their time and energy in sharing their experiences through numerous interviews. I am likewise indebted to a host of central figures who graciously shared their work and life experiences with me, including Stan Sheetz, Charlie Sheetz, Joe Sheetz Jr., Louie Sheetz, and Nancy Sheetz. I am also thankful for the time and generosity of Buddy Casado, Daniel "Chef Dan" Coffin, Jimmy Coonan, Rick Cyman, Stephanie Doliveira, Mike Lorenz, John Mickel, Ray Ryan, Jim Sheetz, Joyce Twombly, Jim Wenner, and Dave "Woody" Woodley, who was such a joy to work with that we conducted the very same interview twice! I am especially thankful to the new generation of Sheetz family members who shared their observations and insights with me, including Adam Sheetz, Ashley Sheetz, Ryan Sheetz, and Travis Sheetz.

For their kind assistance and generosity, I am indebted to a number of folks at Sheetz corporate headquarters and at the company's distribution center, including Bonnie Diehl, Marcia Cahill, Mary Ann Hanlon, Tina Hurm, Deb Kociban, Karen McCabe, Melissa McKee, Valerie Metzler, Barbara Miller, Tyne Palazzi, Gary Partner, Maria Patrick, Jill Reed, Andrea Rogers, Kristin Smith, and Gary Zimmerman. Likewise, a variety of different resources made this book possible, including the *Altoona Mirror*'s Walt Frank, whose Sheetz exposé provided a helpful timeline, along with Arcadia Publishing's Katie Kellett, Abby Henry, Jim Kempert, Rebekah Collinsworth, Erin Vosgien, and Lindsay Carter. Special thanks are due to Tammy Dunkley, the Sheetz corporate advertising manager, for bringing the book's cover art to fruition.

A very special shout-out is due to Nicki Barnes, Steve and Stan's executive assistant at Sheetz, who was an indefatigable source of goodwill and comradeship throughout the composition of this book. I am particularly thankful for the warmth and friendship of Earl Springer, who never failed to answer my queries, no matter how small. Earl, you are made to order indeed!

At Penn State Altoona, I am thankful for the encouragement and support of Lori J. Bechtel-Wherry, Michele Kennedy, Nancy Vogel, and Sue Woodring. Special thanks are due to Roseanna Shumskas for her invaluable assistance and expertise in assembling this book's photographic record. I am especially grateful for the steadfast efforts of Kira Condee-Padunova, my top-drawer research assistant, who transcribed hundreds of hours of interviews in preparation for this book's composition. Finally, I am indebted to my wife, Jeanine Womack, who makes all things possible.

Unless otherwise noted, all images are courtesy of Sheetz.

One

THE FIFTH AVENUE DAIRY

The story of Sheetz—as with the narrative of any successful, long-term venture—has a certain element of risk embedded in it. And for all of his business acumen, Bob Sheetz, the company's founder, has a gambler's persona. Make no mistake about it. He knows how to ride a lucky streak. As his younger brother Louie remarks, "Bob is fearless, very independent. He is a true adventurer."

Bob's brother Steve is fond of recalling an instance in 1971 in which the famous "Pistol Pete" Maravich was playing the sold-out NIT tournament at Madison Square Garden. "Bob and I both love sports," Steve remembers, "and Bob said, 'Let's go.' I said, 'We don't have tickets.' Bob said, 'We're going. Let's go.' He was always that way."

With nothing to lose, the ticketless brothers drove up from Philadelphia to New York City. Standing outside of Madison Square Garden, Steve says, "What do we do?" Without missing a beat, the ever-resourceful Bob begins banging on the arena's door. "We better find someone who'll listen," Bob retorts. Steve still recalls the sound of his older brother knocking on Madison Square Garden's side entrance. "Boom! Boom! Boom! Finally, a guy opens the doors. It's the janitor. Bob says, 'Here. Twenty-dollar bill. Here.' The guy says, 'There's no seats in there.' Bob says, 'I don't care.' Twenty bucks, here we go. We walk right in." Before you know it, Bob and Steve find themselves observing the game from the steps within the arena's upper echelons. The janitor told the Sheetz brothers to return to the sold-out Madison Square Garden on the very next evening, where they watched Lew Alcindor of the Milwaukee Bucks take on Willis Reed and the New York Knicks from a pair of mid-court seats. Not too long after that, Bob and Steve tried their hand at the World Series. And later, at the US Open.

After that, Steve remembers, it was "always last minute. I didn't have to ask again. I knew we didn't have tickets." But the lesson was eminently clear. "When somebody tells you that 'you can't do something,' you can do it," Steve observes. "And Bob gave me that attitude early. Forever after that, I knew you could just do anything. That's when I started saying, 'This is America. You can do anything in America.' "

In itself, the story of Sheetz is a truly American story, dating back to the 19th century and the birth of James E. "J.E." Harshbarger, whose Dutch-born ancestors first immigrated to the United States in the early 1800s. Born on January 7, 1882, at Old Fort in Centre County, Pennsylvania, J.E. was the son of H.K. and Lydia Confer Harshbarger. Known as "Cal," H.K. Harshbarger operated a series of thresher outfits in the Centre Hall area, along with a farm some seven miles from Penn State's University Park campus. With Lydia, he fathered seven children, including William ("Billy"), J.E., Harry, Maxwell, Elsie, Bess, and Frank. At the turn of the 20th century, J.E. moved to Philadelphia, where he studied for a year at the University of Pennsylvania before enrolling in a commercial business course at the Sclussler Business College in Norristown, outside of Philadelphia. J.E. came to adore Philadelphia, which had a population of some 1.3 million people when he first entered its city limits, and he would return to the city as often as he could for the balance of his lifetime.

Having completed his education, J.E. took a position as a bookkeeper in a downtown Philadelphia bank. In spite of his affection for Philadelphia and his new life in the city, J.E. was forced to return to the central Pennsylvania countryside after being diagnosed with an acute allergy to the asbestos that filled the walls and ceilings of the buildings he frequented. The only solution, it seemed, was for J.E. to get outdoors—and quickly, at that. In 1906, he left the city and settled briefly with his older brother Billy, who operated a chicken farm outside of Bellwood, Pennsylvania, about 45 miles away from his old stomping grounds in Centre Hall. Working on Billy's farm allowed J.E.'s health to improve in short order.

In 1906, J.E. also came into the orbit of Jennie MacFarland, the daughter of Albert and Adelaide MacFarland. Albert ran an undertaking business in Bellwood. In addition to his work as funeral director, he also operated a hardware store and a carpentry business where he specialized, not surprisingly, in building caskets. J.E. originally met Jennie, born in Bellwood on November 20, 1882, at one of the regular Friday evening dances held in State College, and on October 27, 1908, they were married. Not long afterwards, J.E. and Jennie set up housekeeping at J.E.'s house at 2410 Fifth Avenue in Altoona, some eight miles south of Bellwood. Together, J.E. and Jennie had seven children, including James E. Jr., Charles Howard, Albert Henry, Roy Willard, Russell Guy, Kathleen, and Marian.

In 1907, J.E.'s fortunes would change forever when he noticed a common and long-standing theme among the Bellwood farming class. The central Pennsylvania dairy farmers were inundated with an overabundance of milk from their dairy cows, and they were in desperate need of a means for transporting their surplus milk into the marketplace. With this concept in mind—along with a growing entrepreneurial streak that he had been nurturing since his days at the University of Pennsylvania—he established the business that would eventually become known as the J.E. Harshbarger Dairy Company. To J.E.'s mind, it made sense to open his business in the city of Altoona, which offered a more central and much larger marketplace than Bellwood.

Indeed, by the 1910 census, Altoona's population would rise above 52,000, placing it among Pennsylvania's most populous cities. By mid-century, the growing burg would rise above 77,000 as the railroad boom reached its apex. The Pennsylvania Railroad originally founded Altoona in 1849 in order to build a shop complex to service the commonwealth's rail industry. Incorporated as a borough in February 1854, the city was named after Altona, the German rail and manufacturing center on the banks of the Elbe. By contrast, popular folklore traces the city's name to a Cherokee derivation of the word *allatoona*.

Regardless of its etymology, Altoona owed its very existence to the construction of the Horseshoe Curve, which was built by the Pennsylvania Railroad between 1851 and 1854 in order to provide a more time-efficient alternative to the Allegheny Portage Railroad, which was the only east-west passage for large transport during that era. By lessening the grade towards the summit of the Allegheny Mountains, the Horseshoe Curve was an engineering marvel, virtually redefining the state's rail industry in the process. By the advent of World War II, the Horseshoe Curve had become such a significant aspect of the nation's infrastructure that Nazi Germany's failed Operation Pastorius identified it as a strategic target. By the 1860s, Altoona was growing at a remarkable rate, largely due to the steady demand for locomotives during the Civil War. The Union held the Loyal War Governors' Conference at Altoona's Logan House Hotel in September 1862 in support of Pres. Abraham Lincoln's landmark Emancipation Proclamation following the Battle of Antietam. By the turn of the 20th century, Altoona had become a key regional transportation hub as well as home to thousands of railroad employees and their families.

In June 1907, J.E. began his dairy operation in this bustling central Pennsylvania city, initially opening up shop in the large garage behind his home on Fifth Avenue. The garage itself opened onto an alley just across from Adams Grade School. Having christened his new business the

Fifth Avenue Dairy, J.E. started out simply. With most homes at this time lacking the necessary refrigeration to prevent spoilage, J.E. enjoyed an eager and ready market. As Bob recalls, "He had a ladle, and the ladle had a hook that would hang inside the can. And J.E. would dish out the milk one can at a time." In those pre-pasteurization days, a dairy distributor like J.E. would transport his product into the city from dairy farms across the region. Every morning at 5:00 a.m., J.E. drove his horse and buggy to the Altoona train station, where he would pick up five-gallon cans of milk from the dairy farmers. With nearly a dozen cans in his buggy, J.E. made his rounds, knocking on his neighbors' doors. Local housewives would emerge from their homes with pans into which J.E. scooped out milk at 2¢ per ladleful. Meanwhile, Jennie catered to customer needs back at the Harshbarger home, where folks from the neighborhood would stop by to pick up their milk. By 11:00 a.m., J.E.'s buggy would be all but empty, and he would return to the train station for a second batch of milk for distribution. As the Fifth Avenue Dairy's business grew, J.E. quickly expanded his route, with Jennie trying her hand at the horse and buggy while her husband increased their customer base by purchasing yet another horse and buggy to establish additional routes across the city.

As a harbinger of things to come, J.E. not only saw his business prosper, but also eagerly embraced the dairy's expansion from its rather humble origins. Indeed, within the next decade, the Fifth Avenue Dairy had grown well beyond the confines of J.E.'s tiny garage. In 1923, the J.E. Harshbarger Dairy Company was born when J.E. built a large dairy processing plant at the corner of Fourth Avenue and Twenty-fourth Street in Altoona. In keeping with his well-known frugal personality, J.E. did not begin construction until he had accumulated enough capital to nearly pay for the two-story brick building outright. As Bob recalls, the new dairy was a state-of-the-art processing facility for its time. "It was the real thing," says Bob. "He had a platform where the dairy workers could load six flatbed trucks in the morning." With the horse and buggy having been superseded by automotive transportation, J.E. was able to rapidly increase productivity. In those pre-regulation days—"You didn't have to keep everything refrigerated and iced and all that," Bob recalls—the Harshbarger Dairy's trucks would leave the Altoona plant at 3:00 a.m. and gather milk from the farmers, who had conveniently built loading platforms of their own in order to expedite the process. In later years, as health standards came into vogue, refrigerated tankers replaced the flatbed trucks. J.E. and Jennie's eldest son Jim, who had earned a degree in dairy husbandry from Penn State University, was placed in charge of ensuring the dairy's compliance with agricultural regulations. Born on July 28, 1909, Jim would periodically visit area farmers to make certain that they were maintaining state-mandated health standards by sanitizing their own processing equipment and conforming to appropriate bacteria counts. By this point, the dairy's business had become so large that the risk of contamination of the company's product was very high—and potentially very costly. As Bob remembers, "If a farmer's milk was tainted, his bacteria went up. When the milk arrived at the dairy, the bacteria from a contaminated batch would pour into the plant's vats and spread very quickly, destroying the entire inventory."

Meanwhile, Jim's younger sister Kathleen, born on April 5, 1912, had begun working at the dairy as a part-time bookkeeper during her teenage years. Working on Saturdays when school was in session, Kathleen enjoyed five-day working weeks during the summer, when she came to learn nearly everything there was to know about the operation of the dairy, eventually rising to the position of treasurer. After graduating from high school, Kathleen enrolled in the Altoona School of Commerce, where she met schoolmate Gerald R. "Jerry" Sheets. Born September 29, 1910, Jerry grew up in Spangler (now Northern Cambria), a coal-mining town some 30 miles northwest of Altoona. The second youngest of 11 children, Jerry was the son of James Sheets (1857–1918), a railroad engineer who regularly traversed the Altoona-Pittsburgh run, and the former Effie Betz (1871–1951). Jerry's father later died of lung disease after having spent much of his life shoveling coal to keep the steam engines running. Jerry's siblings included Charles, Wilhamina, Edith, Walter, Ruth, Arvella, Clara, Lucella, Henry, and Lodema.

After a brief courtship, Jerry and Kathleen married in November 1930 in Cumberland, Maryland. In short order, Jerry took an entry-level position with his new father-in-law's dairy, working as a milk truck driver and making daily deliveries in Altoona. Soon thereafter, Jerry was promoted to route manager before serving as sales manager for the J.E. Harshbarger Dairy Company. Eventually, Jerry "became the fair-haired boy," as Bob recalls, and was promoted to J.E.'s second in command at the dairy, placing him in the challenging political position of being in charge of his five brothers-in-law.

Jerry's swift ascension up the dairy's employment ladder mirrors a transformative period in the life of the plant. By the early 1940s, the dairy had become a lucrative, around-the-clock business, having amassed 42 routes across the region. In addition to a loading platform that could accommodate four trucks at a time, the processing plant featured a complex pasteurization and refrigeration system. After the flatbed trucks returned with their predawn milk pickups from area dairy farms, the raw milk product entered the plant at ground level through a conveyor belt that carried the liquid to a large vat on the second floor for pasteurization. Meanwhile, the dairy's bottling operation was carried out on the first floor. During the evenings, empty bottles would be trucked into the loading dock and transported via a conveyer belt into the plant for sanitization. The clean bottles would then be conveyed beneath the second-floor vat, which, by virtue of gravity, would fill the sanitized bottles through a series of 36 metal teats. The milk would then be transported into the marketplace—largely through home sales, at this time—and the production process would begin anew.

In just two decades, J.E. Harshbarger had virtually remade himself, having taken a backyard dairy business and turned it into a full-fledged regional operation. And with Jerry Sheets as his right-hand man, J.E.'s dairy was destined for even greater heights.

The son of H.K. and Lydia Confer Harshbarger, James E. "J.E." Harshbarger was born on January 7, 1882, at Old Fort in Centre County, Pennsylvania.

Pictured here is J.E. Harshbarger's younger brother Harry, who had a twin brother named Max.

After completing high school, J.E. Harshbarger (front, far left) moved to Philadelphia, where he studied for a year at the University of Pennsylvania before enrolling in a commercial business course at the Sclussler Business College in Norristown. J.E. later took a position as a bookkeeper in a downtown Philadelphia bank.

This is an early photograph of Jennie MacFarland, who was the daughter of Albert and Adelaide MacFarland. Born in Bellwood, Pennsylvania, on November 20, 1882, Jennie met J.E. Harshbarger at one of the regular Friday evening dances held in State College. They married on October 27, 1908.

Jennie's father, Albert MacFarland (left), ran an undertaking business in Bellwood. In addition to his work as funeral director, he also operated a hardware store and a carpentry business where he specialized in building caskets.

Adelaide MacFarland, pictured here, was Jennie's mother.

Lillie MacFarland, Jennie's sister, later married John Price.

Another early photograph of Jennie MacFarland Harshbarger is seen here. Together, J.E. and Jennie had seven children, including James E. Jr., Charles Howard, Albert Henry, Roy Willard, Russell Guy, Kathleen, and Marian.

The son of J.E. and Jennie Harshbarger, Charles Howard Harshbarger was the second eldest of the Harshbarger children.

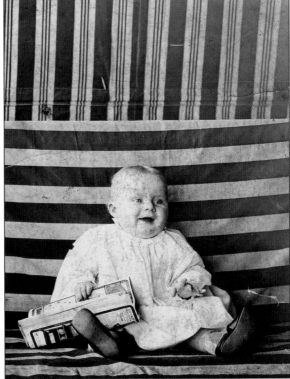

Roy Willard Harshbarger was J.E. and Jennie Harshbarger's fourth child.

Pictured here are, from left to right, Jennie Harshbarger, John's sister Elizabeth, and John Price Jr., son of Jennie's sister Lillie.

Photographed during the late 1920s are Jennie Harshbarger (sitting) along with Walter Fogelsanger of Shippensburg, Pennsylvania, and Blanche Kipple of Juniata, Pennsylvania.

Charles Harshbarger is pictured in his military dress uniform in 1943. In later years, the Sheetz children would come to refer to him as their beloved Uncle Chill.

Shortly after settling in Altoona, J.E. Harshbarger realized that central Pennsylvania dairy farmers were inundated with an overabundance of milk from their dairy cows. To handle the surplus milk and serve this growing market, J.E. opened the Fifth Avenue Dairy, which originally transported its product into the city from dairy farms via horse and buggy.

J.E. Harshbarger is seen at his home at First Avenue and Twenty-fourth Street in Altoona.

The J.E. Harshbarger Dairy is pictured here in 2013. In 1923, the J.E. Harshbarger Dairy Company was born when J.E. built this dairy processing plant at the corner of Fourth Avenue and Twenty-fourth Street in Altoona. There was also a dairy store on the corner of the building where milk and ice cream products were sold. (Photograph by Roseanna Shumskas.)

With the horse and buggy having been superseded by automotive transportation, the Harshbarger Dairy was able to rapidly increase productivity. J.E. and Jennie Harshbarger's son Albert Henry is pictured at left. The wording on the side of the truck celebrates the gold medal that the J.E. Harshbarger Dairy earned for the quality of its product from the Pennsylvania Department of Agriculture.

Quart- and half-pint-sized milk bottles, featuring the distinctive red labels of the J.E. Harshbarger Dairy, are seen here. (Photograph by Kenneth Womack.)

This advertisement is for an open house at the J.E. Harshbarger Dairy in May 1923, when the business was opened to the public for a demonstration of the dairy's brand-new pasteurizing equipment. Pictured are, from left to right, the milk heater, the viscolizer (similar to a low-pressure homogenizer), and the cultured buttermilk machine.

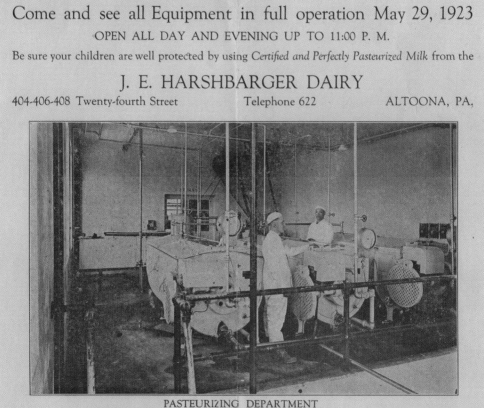

Come and see all Equipment in full operation May 29, 1923

OPEN ALL DAY AND EVENING UP TO 11:00 P. M.

Be sure your children are well protected by using *Certified and Perfectly Pasteurized Milk* from the

J. E. HARSHBARGER DAIRY

404-406-408 Twenty-fourth Street   Telephone 622   ALTOONA, PA.

PASTEURIZING DEPARTMENT
Showing Three Cherry Pasteurizers, Milk Heater, Viscolizer and Cultured Buttermilk Machine

Two

THAT'S SHEETZ—WITH A Z

Having proven himself and earned his way into the managerial ranks of the J.E. Harshbarger Dairy Company, Jerry Sheets began attending dairy industry conferences—another harbinger of things to come. As his wife, Kathleen, later recalled, at one such meeting Jerry dutifully stepped up to the registration table to collect his name tag. He was startled to see two name tags bearing a striking resemblance—his own, embossed with *Jerry Sheets*, and yet another imprinted with the name *Jerry Sheetz*. To Kathleen's great surprise, Jerry pondered each name tag before selecting the latter. "What are you doing?" she asked. "I like this one better," he replied. "But that's not your name!" she protested. "Maybe so," he answered. "But I like the z. I think we're going to change our name." Aghast, Kathleen observed, "You don't just change your name!" Over the next several years, Jerry, unwavering in his quest, went through the painstaking process of altering his surname, eventually traveling from Altoona to Harrisburg, the state capital, in order to procure a new birth certificate. As Kathleen remembered, "We were fighting for five or six years, but he was determined to change the name."

For years, Jerry staved off the criticisms of his siblings, who thought he was crazy to change their birth name. "I like it better," he would confidently tell them, having become resolute in his decision. According to Bob, the roots of the family surname's terminal z may have also been the product of cultural aspirations towards upward mobility. As Bob remembers, in Spangler, where Jerry grew up, the population grew to 7,500 people, along with a thriving downtown fueled by an influx of European immigrants. "My father knew the Jewish bankers and merchants there," Bob recalls, "and many of their last names ended with z. My father said, 'I'm going to be a businessman, too, and I'm going to end my name with a z.'" Regardless of the surname's origins, the name *Sheetz* would have far-reaching implications—not to mention a natural pizzazz that could be ideal, given the right context, for marketing purposes.

For Jerry and Kathleen, family life revolved around the dairy, with Jerry managing the plant and Kathleen having served as treasurer. The Sheetz family dinner table was consumed with stories about the dairy. And why not? The business was filled with larger-than-life characters such as Uncle Albie, Kathleen's irascible brother. When he was not at the dairy, Albie spent most of his time at Ajay's (now Jack and George's), the bar across the street from the plant. As Steve recalls, Albie and the other characters at the dairy would leave bags of chocolate candy for the Sheetz children in the family's milk box after a night of carousing at Ajay's. Sometimes, Albie's hard-drinking ways spilled over into the dairy, where he worked as a bottle cleaner on the first floor. Every so often, Albie would light a firecracker inside one of the empty milk bottles and startle the staff—save for the usually staid J.E., that is, who could not resist laughing at his employee's earthy ways. On another infamous occasion, Albie absconded with one of the dairy's trucks, which he drove up to Tyrone for a night of debauchery. The next day, the truck was still in Tyrone, some 18 miles north of the city, while a heavily inebriated Albie was sitting on the floor of the dairy, wondering how he managed to make his way back to Altoona without his ride.

During this same period, Jerry and Kathleen's immediate family was growing quickly, with eight children born between 1932 and 1955. After an infant son died shortly after childbirth—he would have been christened Gerald Jr.—the Sheetz children included James (born June 21, 1932), Gerald Robert (November 1, 1934), Nancy (May 20, 1938), Marjorie (January 25, 1942), Joseph (October 11, 1945), Stephen (January 7, 1948), Charles (April 4, 1952), and Randall [Louie] (May 30, 1955). Jerry and Kathleen raised their growing brood at the family home located at Second Avenue and Twenty-fourth Street in Altoona. For the young Sheetz family, life was firmly centered around activities associated with church and work. As Steve recalls, "Our mother and father were very religious. Every Sunday we had to go to church—*had* to go to church! I'd always try to hide under the pillow, and my father would come and get mad, and then we'd have to go. Dad would drive his Cadillac down to Simpson Methodist, and we'd always go to the same pew. It was the Sheetz pew, up at the right front of the church." After church, Jerry and Kathleen established a routine in which the family would take groceries and dairy goods to widows, shut-ins, and other less-fortunate people around the city. Jerry and Kathleen ingrained this sense of charity in their children. As Steve recalls, as a church deacon, "Jerry would learn about various people in need, and he would take it upon himself to help them out. At the dairy, we used to gather quarts of eggnog and ice cream to share with folks at Christmastime."

Jerry was equally serious about instilling a work ethic in his children. As Steve remembers, Jerry's philosophy was remarkably simple: "You're 12 years old, you got to go to work. I want you to learn what it's like to go to work, to make money." As with his siblings before him, Steve initially went to work at the dairy. "Our father always wanted us up early in the summer," Steve recalls, and "he would tell us that 'you still have time to play baseball if you want to do it in the afternoon.'" Charlie remembers working in the dairy's ice cream department under his older brother Joe's tutelage: "I was just a laborer at first, packaging up the ice cream for delivery and cleaning up the facilities. Eventually, I learned how to run the whole department, learning a little bit of everything until I knew the plant inside and out." For Steve and Charlie's elder brother Bob, working at the dairy had very different implications. In 1943, Bob began accompanying his father to work at the dairy at the tender age of eight years old. Although he did not know it at the time, Bob later realized that "I was earning my master's degree in the dairy business."

For the lion's share of the next seven years—on most weekends and virtually whenever school was out—Bob joined his father and grandfather in the second-floor business offices of the J.E. Harshbarger Dairy Company. At first, Bob busied himself with coloring books while J.E. and Jerry managed the dairy. But soon, Bob began to take notice of the plant's internal business dynamics, particularly the manner in which his father and grandfather would fine-tune their efforts in concert with shifts in the market. From Bob's vantage point at his desk in the second-floor office, he would observe J.E., who steadfastly kept track of the goings-on in the nearby checkout room, where the drivers would return at various intervals after running the company's 42 routes. Upon their arrival, each driver was required to record all of their sales, and Bob's grandfather was keenly aware of any fluctuations in their local market, no matter how subtle. Meanwhile, Jerry sat at a larger desk nearby, facing J.E., as well as a window into the stairwell, which would allow him to keep track of the dairy's personnel.

As Bob recalls, "I listened to my father and my grandfather together every day. I'd listen to them make decisions about how they'd run the dairy. At the age of 10, I started to think of what they were talking about and how I would do things differently." By the age of 12, Bob adds, "I could predict what they were going to say, and I knew how they were going to react to a given situation." For J.E. and Jerry, these situations invariably involved sales information that they gleaned from their truck drivers. Based upon this intelligence, they discovered that they could improve sales and the dairy's profit margins by making subtle changes in their routes, the dairy's line of products, and the production process itself. Looking back on his experience at the dairy, Bob realized that J.E. and Jerry complemented each other's strengths. "My grandfather," says Bob, "was highly educated. He was a tough businessman, and he was very tough on his employees because he knew right from wrong. Meanwhile, my father, in spite of his lack of education, knew how to keep things running smoothly around the dairy. He also admired my grandfather for his accomplishments and learned a lot from him. In their own ways, they learned a lot from each other."

Not surprisingly, by the early 1940s, J.E. and Jerry had navigated the J.E. Harshbarger Dairy Company into becoming the largest producing dairy in central Pennsylvania. Recognizing that Harshbarger's had become the largest dairy outfit between Pittsburgh and Philadelphia, supermarket giant A&P entered into an exclusive contract with the dairy. At the time, A&P enjoyed strong sales in Altoona and the surrounding area. The conglomerate even operated a large warehouse near the railroad tracks adjacent to Altoona's Twenty-ninth Street bridge. In an effort to make its business more efficient—especially in terms of stemming inventory shortages and product pilferage—A&P approached the dairy about becoming its exclusive vendor. As Bob recalls, A&P stated: "We only want to sell two kinds of milk. We want to sell Harshbarger's milk and a private label, and you're going to bottle both of them." With the A&P contract in place, the company's volume increased substantially, pushing the dairy's capacity to the limit. And Bob witnessed every aspect of the transaction and its aftermath. "I got to observe all of this," he remembers. "I got to hear the decisions being made. I got to see what part of it worked. What part wasn't working."

The dairy's landmark contract with A&P's supermarkets also spelled the end, slowly but surely, of home milk delivery. Indeed, at the beginning of the 1940s, home delivery dominated the industry; by the early 1990s, it made up less than one percent of the market. "It simply became too expensive," Bob notes. "You couldn't have the driver stop the truck in order to carry two quarts of milk up to a house, take the empties back to the dairy" and then continue with a designated supermarket route, where the dairy realized its profit margin. For his part, Jerry was becoming keenly aware of dramatic shifts in the dairy market, especially in regard to retail distribution. As the dairy's de facto director of sales and marketing, Jerry naturally began "thinking about how to create more sales because area supermarkets were gradually extending their hours," says Bob, yet "they weren't open on Sundays because of Pennsylvania's blue laws." Originally passed in 1794 at the height of the state's Quaker influence and designed to enforce religious standards, the commonwealth's blue laws prohibited the operation of retail stores, including grocery stores, on Sundays; in later years, the laws were considered to be a secular virtue because they protected Sunday as a designated day for rest and preserving family unity. By the 1970s, blue laws would slowly begin to be repealed across the United States.

But in the interim, Jerry saw the blue laws as an opportunity to create a unique Sunday marketplace in order to provide families with much-needed weekend dairy products. With the shrinking home-delivery market, he also recognized that the future of the dairy business required the establishment of more—as opposed to fewer—distribution possibilities in the era of large supermarket conglomerates like A&P. At the same time, Jerry noted the increasing market share enjoyed by the Johnstown Sani-Dairy—which sold dairy novelty items such as the Creamsicle— and Howard Johnson's, the restaurant chain that had recently opened a franchise in nearby Hollidaysburg and was nationally known for its soda fountain and ice cream fare. Recognizing that his frugal father-in-law was unlikely to invest in the equipment to rival the operations of outfits like the Johnstown Sani-Dairy and Howard Johnson's, Jerry decided to open up a dairy store of his own. As Bob recalls, Jerry was eager to enter the market, announcing that "we've got to build some of our own outlets."

To this end, Jerry opened the inaugural Sheetz Dairy Store in 1941. Located at 2601 Fifth Avenue at the Union Avenue intersection in Altoona (now the offices of magisterial district judge Todd F. Kelly), Jerry's first outlet specialized, not surprisingly, in milk and ice cream. His initial investment involved an ice cream maker known as a batch machine because it could produce five gallons at a time. As Steve recalls, Jerry opened four more stores in 1942, including locations on Fourth

Street, Tenth Street, Second Avenue in the city's Juniata neighborhood, and Broad Avenue and Twenty-fourth Street. "He opened five dairy stores in total," says Steve, "just like that."

Before long, the United States entered World War II, and sugar rationing ensued. For Jerry, the scarcity of sugar created an unexpected sales boon after the dairy began using marshmallow as the sweetener for the company's ice cream mixture. Suddenly, the Sheetz Dairy Stores could barely keep ice cream in stock. For the next few years, virtually nobody else sold ice cream in the region. Jerry specialized in vanilla, chocolate, and chocolate chip ice cream. For a while, he toyed with a teaberry flavor, but it hardly mattered, Bob remembers, because in those sugar-rationing days "you could sell everything you could make! And when you're selling everything you make, you bump the price up a little, and suddenly you're making a lot of money!"

But Jerry's success with the Sheetz Dairy Store was to be short-lived. By the mid-1940s, Bob notes, the war had ended, sugar rationing had ceased, "and business went to hell." Quite suddenly, the Sheetz Dairy Store was no longer the only ice cream game in town. To Bob's mind, Jerry's success occurred entirely because he was responding to demand without being prepared to respond to a changing, competitive market. In truth, Bob observes, Jerry "was making money, but he wasn't really a store operator. He was a dairy man—and there's a world of difference." During the war, "it was so easy! He was making a ton of money without doing anything. All of a sudden, he had to become an operator, but he didn't know how to operate stores!"

At the same time, Bob's own life was awash in a sea of changes. At 15, he left the dairy to work in Jerry's flagging outlet at Fifth and Union Avenues. He worked there after school and on weekends, and, as with the Harshbarger dairy, he soon knew the business inside and out. After his public education came to an end in the spring of 1952, Bob tried his hand for a semester at Penn State University's nearby Altoona campus, but his life changed in a hurry after his high school sweetheart Nancy Hicks (born July 9, 1935) became pregnant. At 18 years of age with a baby on the way and having just graduated from Altoona Area High School, Bob needed to chart a course for his life—and in a hurry, no less.

Yet in sharp contrast with many of his relatives, Bob did not see his future at the J.E. Harshbarger Dairy Company. As it so happened, Bob had very different ideas in mind. And with his gambler's persona in full flower, he was ready and poised to ride that lucky streak.

Effie Sheets is pictured here around 1899. With husband James Sheets, a railroad engineer, the former Effie Betz had 11 children, including Charles, Wilhamina, Edith, Walter, Ruth, Arvella, Clara, Lucella, Henry, Gerald, and Lodema.

Henry and Jerry Sheets (right) are seen here as children. Born on September 29, 1910, Gerald R. "Jerry" Sheets grew up in Spangler (now Northern Cambria), Pennsylvania, a coal-mining town some 30 miles northwest of Altoona.

Pictured are Jerry Sheets and Kathleen Harshbarger in April 1930. Born on April 5, 1912, J.E. and Jennie Harshbarger's daughter Kathleen had begun working at the dairy as a part-time bookkeeper during her teenage years, eventually rising to the position of treasurer. After graduating from high school, Kathleen enrolled in the Altoona School of Commerce, where she met schoolmate Jerry Sheets, whom she married in November 1930 after a brief courtship.

This early photograph shows Jerry and Kathleen Sheets. Together, Jerry and Kathleen had eight children, including James, Robert ("Bob"), Nancy, Marjorie, Joseph, Stephen, Charles, and Randall ("Louie").

Albert Harshbarger—the Sheetz children's fun-loving, irascible Uncle Albie—worked the Harshbarger Dairy's bottle-cleaning equipment.

Pictured in this early photograph is Bob Sheetz (center) with older brother Jim and cousin Shirley Havlin.

The Sheetz family home is pictured in 2013 at Second Avenue and Twenty-fourth Street in Altoona. (Photograph by Roseanna Shumskas.)

Jerry Sheetz is pictured here with his daughter Nancy.

Under the Sheetz®
Zuper Ztrategy
Tears Up Old
Industry Thinking

In 1931, Jerry Sheets would rechristen the family surname as *Sheetz* after attending a dairy industry conference. The name *Sheetz* would have far-reaching implications, not to mention a natural pizzazz—as the cover of the July 1998 issue of *CSP* (the magazine for convenience store people) demonstrates—that would prove to be ideal for marketing purposes.

Three

DRIVEN TO WIN

For Bob Sheetz, the answer to his immediate problems was simple: he was determined to buy his father's Fifth Avenue Sheetz Dairy Store and turn it into a profitable venture. And he knew exactly how he would bring his dream to fruition, having served his business apprenticeship nestled between his father and grandfather in the second-floor offices of the J.E. Harshbarger Dairy Company.

But buying the store from his father would be another matter altogether. Jerry Sheetz was convinced that the slumping store had become a lost cause; that it had long since faded from the profitability that it enjoyed during its brief World War II heyday. "I told my father the changes I wanted to make," Bob recalls, and "he said the store never showed a profit." Jerry counseled his son to dismiss the idea out of hand. "I can't make any money at that store!" he pleaded with Bob. "It doesn't do enough business!" In this fashion, Jerry attempted, with great earnestness, to talk his son out of buying the store, but Bob would not be deterred. "[My father] tried with all his power to discourage me," Bob remembers, but in the well-honed spirit of his frugal-minded grandfather J.E., Bob was prepared to put cash on the nail. "I had a lot of money at that time," Bob recalls. "I had saved nearly a thousand bucks." At the time, Bob had accumulated $990 in his savings account in Altoona's First National Bank. He withdrew the balance and presented it to Jerry, who—realizing that his son simply could not be dissuaded—suggested that Bob pay $900 to purchase the Fifth Avenue Sheetz Dairy Store's inventory, while renting the building and its equipment from his father. "You keep the $90 that's left," Jerry told him. "You will need it for cash to open the next day."

To Bob's mind, the Sheetz Dairy Store's location was ideal. Situated on a five-point intersection, the store had two entrances, with foot traffic strolling in from nearby homes and merchants. "But most of my business," Bob recalls, "was automobiles pulling in off of Union Avenue and off of Fifth Avenue to my side entrance." Bob also desired the location because it existed at a key junction between the city's business district and its residential neighborhoods. "If you worked anywhere in downtown Altoona, whether it was retail, wholesale, or manufacturing," Bob reasons, "chances are you went home on Union Avenue."

And as he had alluded to his father, Bob had big plans for radically shifting the Sheetz Dairy Store's "offer," industry shorthand for a business's retail product mix. Bob planned to diversify the existing store's dairy-outlet focus and supplement it with a range of deli, grocery, and convenience items. "I was so sales oriented," Bob remembers. "I had specials going on all the time." By increasing the store's offer, he intended to adhere to the old sales maxim of "pile it high—watch it fly." Bob proposed to accomplish this through the tried-and-true method of growing the flagging dairy store's customer volume.

The concept of Bob's volume-oriented sales approach is, in and of itself, the cornerstone of the convenience store retail offer. As an industry, convenience stores typically date their historical beginnings to 1927, when the Southland Ice Company, which later grew into the behemoth 7-Eleven chain, opened a storefront in Dallas, Texas. John Jefferson Green, an employee of Southland Ice Company, began selling milk, eggs, and bread in one of the company's icehouses, drawing upon the ice plant's cooling facilities to preserve his products' freshness. As the success of Green's efforts began to build, the icehouse's manager, Joe C. "Jodie" Thompson Jr., opened additional locations, eventually transforming the Southland Ice Company into the Southland Corporation, which operated several locations throughout the greater Dallas area.

While the Great Depression forced the company into bankruptcy in 1931, the Southland Corporation enjoyed a retail boom during the postwar years. In 1946, the business was re-branded as 7-Eleven in order to connote the convenience stores' hours of operation—7:00 a.m. to 11:00 p.m.—which were extraordinary business hours during that era. By 1952, when Bob purchased the Sheetz Dairy Store from his father, 7-Eleven had opened its 100th location. In 1962, 7-Eleven opened its first 24-hour location in Austin, Texas, and within the following year began transforming nearly all of its convenience stores into 24-hour businesses. As with other convenience operations, 7-Eleven offered an array of dairy items, bread, soft drinks, eggs, coffee, candy products, doughnuts, canned goods, and newspapers. In 1966, the convenience store industry notched $1 billion in sales for the first time. By the end of the decade, the industry had grown precipitously, having surpassed more than $3.5 billion in annual sales.

When Bob first opened the Sheetz Dairy Store on November 1, 1952, he made several radical changes in short order. "I saw what worked and didn't work, how they handled people. I got to see all of that at a young age," he recalls. "When I took over, I wanted to make changes. I changed the structure of the business." To this end, he realized that he needed to change the store's retail offer in a hurry. "I piled everything high," Bob remembers. "I wanted to sell everything, and I was selling stuff at cost. I wanted customers in the store." With his new sales plan at the ready, Bob engaged in a full-court press involving new product arrays, special sales promotions, and an advertising scheme. Bob enlivened the Sheetz Dairy Store's offer by providing chipped ham that he shipped in from Dubuque, Iowa. The ham arrived in eight-pound cans, and the contents had to be processed through a gravity-fed meat slicer. "On a good Sunday," Bob points out, "I could sell 10 cases of that. Four hundred and eighty pounds, we could sell on a Sunday. Many times, I sold at cost. I just wanted traffic."

Bob supplemented his chipped ham sales with fresh bread from Haller's Eagle Bakery, located about a dozen blocks away from the dairy store on Fifth Avenue. Bob also provided his customers with French-stick baguettes. As Bob recalls, "You could get eight French sticks to a flat box, and the box had indentations around it so you could stack them without smashing them. Haller's started to bring that in and, boy, I saw how good it was. It was full of flavor, and so I ordered 20 the very first day, and we sold out in no time." With the success of his two new food items, Bob began contemplating his price points in order to maximize his profit. He began by negotiating with the bakery, which started opening up on Sundays in order to prepare 1,000 fresh loaves for delivery to the Sheetz Dairy Store. Taking advantage of existing blue laws, Bob began to shift the sales price of his product line in order to create special sales promotions and improve his margin. For example, Bob notes that the French stick "sold for 15 cents and I paid 12 cents. I raised the chipped ham by 10 cents a pound, and if you bought half a pound I gave you a free French stick." Pretty soon, customers were buying half-pound quantities of chipped ham in order to earn the free baguette. On some Sundays, Bob would reward customers who purchased a half-pound or more of chipped ham with a free copy of the *Pittsburgh Press*, which retailed for 15¢. Before long, Bob's Sunday business alone was turning over nearly 500 pounds of chipped ham, 600 copies of the *Pittsburgh Press*, and 1,000 French sticks.

"I had real traffic now," Bob recalls. "I just wanted the volume. I wanted them to buy another item. Two items, three. Whatever I could sell them. Everything else in the store was marked up high. But I had to have that sales leader—whether it was the chipped ham, the *Pittsburgh Press*, or the French stick." To create his sales leaders, Bob promoted the Sheetz Dairy Store's product line in the *Altoona Mirror*, which enjoyed a daily circulation in the early 1950s of approximately 35,000 copies. "Their back page was the most effective advertising anywhere," Bob remembers, "and advertising was always by the column. What they pushed was one column, four inches." Working with Jim Sidle, the newspaper's advertising salesman, Bob negotiated for three columns' worth of advertising space. "If you'll buy three columns," Jim retorted, "you can have a square—six inches by six inches. You can have the top right-hand corner." Suddenly, the Sheetz Dairy Store had a standing advertisement space of its own in the region's most circulated daily newspaper. For Bob, it was nothing short of "a godsend."

With his Sunday business growing at an impressive pace, Bob desperately needed to add to his employee base. When he purchased the Sheetz Dairy Store from his father, he continued the employment of Sue Cirelli, an ice cream maker by trade. As Bob recalls, "She was working for my father eight hours a day, and so I determined the hours I needed her" in order to maintain the store's ice cream production. Bob also kept Sue on staff because he supplemented his own income from the store as a school bus driver in order to support his growing family. Bob earned $125 a month driving the school bus, which he drove from 6:30 to 8:30 every morning before opening the dairy store at 9:00 a.m.

During this period, Bob and his wife, Nancy, whom he married in 1952, lived briefly in East Freedom, some 14 miles away from Altoona, with Bob's new in-laws, Paul and Edna Hicks. As their young family grew, Bob and Nancy relocated to Altoona, where they lived near J.E. Harshbarger's huge redbrick house at the corner of First Avenue and Twenty-fourth Street. Nearby, at the corner of Second Avenue and Twenty-fourth Street, an Altoona surgeon owned a large stone home with a carriage house, a former horse stable that Bob's parents had purchased in 1945. For the next several years, Bob and Nancy lived in the carriage house, along with their family, which grew to include Jenny (born March 18, 1954), Stan (May 26, 1955), Elizabeth (September 6, 1956), and Polly (April 19, 1960).

Meanwhile, as Bob's business developed, he shrewdly sought out mentors in order to grow his retail knowledge. For Bob, one of his most important early mentors was Ernest E. "Ernie" Wissinger (1906–2002), who operated Wissinger's Markets—later sold to Gateway Foods and reopened as Martin's—in the Altoona area. "He was tough," Bob recalls. "He was probably the best operator I ever met. A great store operator." Bob marveled at Ernie's ability to build and maintain his customer base. "He knew how to do it," says Bob. "He had customers at his original store on Thirty-first Street who used to come from 25 and 30 miles away because he knew how to market merchandise." More importantly, Ernie "did everything right," Bob adds. "He hired good people. He trained them to take care of his customers. On Friday and Saturday nights, he would stand by the cash register and work as a bag boy himself. He would carry bags out to his customers' cars so he could talk to them and thank them personally for coming to his store."

When it came time to hire his own employees, Bob found that he, too, excelled at hiring good people. As it turned out, one of his first employees, John Mickel, went on to become—and, indeed, still is—the company's longest tenured employee. In 1956, Bob hired 15-year-old John to clean the windows and scrub the floors at the Sheetz Dairy Store. As John remembers, "A neighbor, Margaret Harshbarger, said Bob was looking for a stock boy, so I went up, and he hired me. I just wanted a job to make money. I wanted to save money to buy my first car." In no time, Bob discovered that John was "dedicated and loyal. Never once can I remember him saying 'no' to any request I ever made of him. He worked right beside me, 16 hours a day. He wouldn't leave until I would." After handling the store's maintenance and stocking duties, John was surprised when Bob asked him if he had a white shirt. As John recalls, Bob said, " 'Go get it, and I will teach you how to run the store.' He taught me how to wait on people and make change. That is how I learned how to be a manager. A few years later, I became manager of the store," John adds. Like his own mentor Ernie, Bob was already sharing the knowledge that he had gleaned as a young businessman.

For his own part, Bob's early years at the Sheetz Dairy Store were an exhilarating time. "I loved what I was doing so much, and it was such a challenge to me," Bob remembers. "I couldn't wait to get to work every day. I loved what I was doing." And the success he was enjoying at the former dairy outlet was icing on the cake. During his first year of business, the store's sales totaled $36,000, with the second year's receipts growing to $77,000. By the third year, the Sheetz Dairy Store cleared more than $100,000 in sales, validating Bob's instincts about the store's capacity for achieving success. As Bob points out, "At first, I only wanted that one store, that one chance to prove myself. I knew what I could do with that one. I knew the location was good. I was always open seven days a week from day one. I used to listen to the customers' needs. I did most of the rings at the cash register. I knew everybody." And for the Sheetz Dairy Store, that made all the difference.

By far, the cornerstone of Bob's success during this era was the manner in which he parlayed his Sunday business, when the blue laws kept the large-scale supermarkets in check, into a sales phenomenon. As Steve later recalled, "Bob could do five times a normal day on a Sunday. It was unreal. I still remember that I would work part-time in the store, and we'd have French stick bread that'd be hot. The bakery would bring them in, and people would come in for them, and we'd have papers just stacked, hundreds of copies of the *Pittsburgh Press* and *New York Times*. We were the only game in town! *Everybody* came to us, and we couldn't help but say, 'Wow, what are we gonna do next?'"

For Bob, the renaissance of the Sheetz Dairy Store was the express result of his boundless competitive nature. "I was the most competitive guy you would be around in your life," he admits. "I had to be the best. If I wasn't, I drove everyone crazy until I got better at it. I was definitely driven to win. I thrived on competition. I wanted to give our customers a better offer than our competitors." Steve underscores his brother's competitive instincts, adding that "of all the qualities he had, the most important was he was driven to win, and there was no stopping him." No matter what the obstacles happened to be, Steve adds, Bob always "found a way." And the Sheetz Dairy Store, as it turns out, was only just the beginning

Located at 2601 Fifth Avenue at the Union Avenue intersection in Altoona (now the present-day offices of magisterial district judge Todd F. Kelly), the first Sheetz Dairy Store under Bob Sheetz's ownership opened on November 1, 1952. Bob paid his father $900 for the inventory of the Sheetz Dairy Store, leaving him with $90. "You keep the $90 that's left," Jerry Sheetz told his son. "You will need it for cash to open the next day." The store was later renamed Sheetz Kwik Shopper.

In this exterior photograph of Bob Sheetz's first store, a sign advertising chipped ham from Dubuque, Iowa, is visible. "On a good Sunday," Bob later recalled, "I could sell 10 cases of that. Four hundred and eighty pounds, we could sell on a Sunday. Many times, I sold at cost. I just wanted traffic." The photograph was taken at the corner of Union Avenue, Fifth Avenue, and Twenty-sixth Street in Altoona.

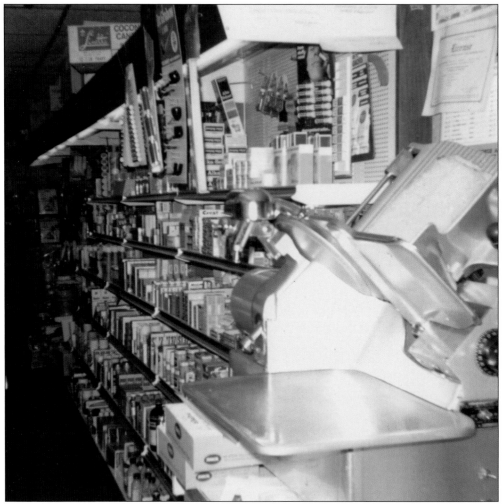
The meat slicer Bob Sheetz used to prepare his bestselling Dubuque chipped ham is pictured here.

In this interior photograph of the first store, Bob Sheetz's array of grocery items is on full display. Taking advantage of existing blue laws, Bob provided consumers with household foodstuffs on Sundays, when area supermarkets were closed.

John Mickel (right) is pictured with Paul Yohe. In 1956, Bob hired 15-year-old John to clean the windows and scrub the floors at the Sheetz Dairy Store. As John remembers, "A neighbor, Margaret Harshbarger, said Bob was looking for a stock boy, so I went up, and he hired me. I just wanted a job to make money. I wanted to save money to buy my first car."

As one of the first employees of Bob Sheetz's inaugural Sheetz Dairy Store location, John Mickel went on to become the company's longest tenured employee. Mickel still frequents the halls of Sheetz headquarters, often overseeing mailroom operations and sharing his wealth of experiences with the company.

Beverly Hargreaves was an early employee of Bob Sheetz's first Sheetz Dairy Store location. Copies of the *Pittsburgh Press* are visible in the foreground.

Altoona mayor Bill Stouffer is seen here with Nancy Boling, Bob's younger sister.

Four

"OPERATING BY THE SEAT OF MY PANTS"

For Bob Sheetz, the impressive early success of the Sheetz Dairy Store was not only a harbinger of things to come, it was also the express result of an ambition that he had nurtured since he opened up that first location back in November 1952—he did not merely want to own the Fifth Avenue location, he wanted to operate an entire retail chain of convenience stores. And true to form, he made no secret about his plans. As Bob remembers, "After I had the first store, I knew I wanted 10. Before I ever opened the 10th, I told my banker, 'I want 100.' And he just cringed."

As the 1950s wore on, Bob began to realize that, in his own words, he had been "operating by the seat of my pants." Always eager to learn as much as he possibly could about retail sales, Bob increased his circle of mentors, which already included his father, Jerry, and Ernie Wissinger. Chief among his growing array of advisors was Phil Klevan (1896–1985), the owner of Klevan Brothers Shoe Stores, and Leo J. Wachter Sr. (1913–1985), an influential member of the board of directors for the First National Bank of Altoona. With his chain of shoe stores, Phil had achieved considerable success and had accrued numerous locations in the mid-Atlantic region. On Monday evenings during the late 1950s, Phil took to closing up shop in his downtown Altoona shoe store and winding up the night in Bob's Fifth Avenue store. "He would stay with me until midnight," Bob remembers. "He would sit, I'd feed him coffee, and he would talk to me and tell me how he grew his business. I'm pretty young at the time, I'm in my early 20s, and I've got a man like this willing to spend time with me. He was my mentor for a long time."

In addition to Phil's indelible influence on Bob's early yen for expansion, Leo Wachter exerted a significant impact upon the young entrepreneur's emerging thought processes about the necessity of financial capital and credit as means for growing his business. To compound his influence, Leo happened to be the president of the tri-county Pepsi distributorship known as the Penn Alto Bottling Works, one of Bob's regular suppliers. Leo served as a board member with the First National Bank of Altoona, and when sales at the Sheetz Dairy Store began to climb, Leo took particular notice. As Bob recalls, "Leo just came out to the store one day and introduced himself, making himself available to me. He taught me about borrowing money. He believed in capital improvements, capital expenditures, how to grow a business." Most importantly, Bob observes, "I had all of these guys ready and willing to advise me. And Leo helped me as much as anyone because he got my credit turned on at First National Bank. Anytime I wanted a loan, he said, 'You tell me what you're going to do, put it on paper, and let me review it.' I went through five straight years where they never turned me down for a loan." Thinking back about Leo's influence, Bob observes, "Leo knew how to finesse. He was really, really good at presenting what he wanted to ultimately achieve. He knew how to get it and helped me learn how to get it."

As one of his earliest capital improvements to the Sheetz Dairy Store, Bob transformed his father's former storage room at the Fifth Avenue location into a restaurant. Dubbing it Bob's Dairy Dine, the eatery operated as a kind of neighborhood deli, with Bob serving as a short-order cook along with his aunt, Bess Franks. In no time flat, Bob's Dairy Dine became the stomping ground for a host of regular customers. As Bob remarks, at Bob's Dairy Dine "you could have ham and eggs, toast and coffee, and pastries from Shirley's Doughnuts," a bakery located in nearby Duncansville. "They made doughnuts fresh every day," Bob recalls. "I had a lot of Shirley's Doughnuts. I probably served two, three dozen a day. Cream-filled mostly. I had a Coca-Cola dispenser, too, where you could draw your own ice." But Bob's secret weapon was Aunt Bess. With her convivial personality, Bob notes, "she could fill that diner. She was friendly, so sweet, the nicest person you'd ever meet on this earth. She was the salt of the earth." A natural cook, Bess often worked without benefit of recipes. "She could make anything you could imagine," says Bob. "She would arrive at work and announce that 'I'm going to make a double-layer cake today. Let's make it chocolate with chocolate icing.' She'd just roll up her sleeves, gather up the ingredients, and dump them in!"

And of course, Bob's Dairy Dine specialized in sandwiches made with the ever-popular Dubuque chipped ham. As Steve remembers, "That was the big seller. The deli was really the business, but it was also built around take home sales, so we had a lot of milk, a lot of ice cream, a lot of grocery items. Aunt Bess would make hoagies and potato salad that we would sell in the restaurant and, for take-home customers, right next to the checkout counter." The formula was simple: customers craved the Sheetz Dairy Store's product line, and Bob's Dairy Dine notched yet another early success. It was none other than Ray Kroc—the entrepreneur behind the global fast-food phenomenon of McDonald's—who argued that the first rule of thumb is to "provide food that customers love, day after day after day. People just want more of it."

As Bob added each new innovation to his offer—the Dubuque chipped ham, the French stick bread, and now Bob's Dairy Dine—his customer base continued to expand, and with the arrival of the 1960s, the Sheetz Dairy Store continued to thrive. The advent of the new decade brought a number of changes, most notably a new employee in the form of Bob's 12-year-old younger brother Steve, who joined his older sisters Nancy and Marjorie by providing part-time help at the store. As with his other siblings, Steve was steeped in his father's work ethic. When he was 11 years old, Steve tried his hand working at the J.E. Harshbarger Dairy Company for a few weeks, filling in with odd jobs and assisting one of the truck drivers. With Jerry running the dairy along with his eldest son Jim, family life at the Sheetz household still revolved around the processing plant. But by this juncture, the dairy store had become equally pervasive in their collective lives. Even holiday gatherings began to conform to the store's hours of operation, with family members either working 8:00 a.m. to 4:00 p.m. or 4:00 p.m. to midnight shifts. As Steve recalls, "I always remember that when mom served Thanksgiving or Christmas dinner it was from 3 to 5. It was almost like a buffet because in those days so many of us had to get back to work at Bob's store."

After completing the seventh grade in June 1960, Steve began working at the Sheetz Dairy Store, putting in some 25 hours a week throughout the summer months. Steve's starting wage was 80¢ an hour; at the end of each week, Bob paid his younger brother with a crisp $20 bill. But Steve was not complaining: "That was a big deal—20 bucks—back then."

In 1962, Bob's dreams of expansion finally came to fruition with the opening of a second store at the corner of Pleasant Valley Boulevard and Twenty-third Street near the campus of Altoona's Bishop Guilfoyle High School. With his new store in the offing, Bob re-branded his chain as Sheetz Kwik Shopper. Not long afterwards, he shuttered Bob's Dairy Dine in order to increase his inventory space and stock additional grocery items, mainly soda and chips. Yet the closing of Bob's interior restaurant hardly brought an end to his deli business. On the contrary, he actually succeeded in expanding his offer by providing customers with more take-home foods and a broader array of groceries. To accomplish this, Bob remodeled the original location yet again, transforming the store's dining facilities into a walk-in cooler and building a kitchen and food-preparation area. From the 1960s through the completion of the Sheetz Distribution Center in 2001, the company procured its grocery items through Economy Wholesale Grocery, a local cooperative. In the early years, Economy Wholesale Grocery would fully stock a new store, and Bob would pay $100 weekly installments until the initial outlay was paid off.

Not surprisingly, Bob mimicked the original store's retail offer at the Sheetz Kwik Shopper's Pleasant Valley Boulevard location. As one of the city's key north-south thoroughfares, Pleasant Valley Boulevard—like Union Avenue—provided customers with ready access to Altoona's business district and a number of residential pockets. The second store was also ideally situated adjacent to Bishop Guilfoyle High School, which afforded Bob a ready clientele when school was in session.

On one unforgettable occasion, though, the Sheetz Kwik Shopper's proximity to the high school resulted in near calamity. The incident involved a district basketball championship game between Bishop Guilfoyle and their Johnstown rivals, Bishop McCort. As it happens, Bishop Guilfoyle did not have any refreshments on hand. When the halftime bell rang, the game's announcer naturally directed attendees to the nearby Sheetz Kwik Shopper for a quick snack before the resumption of the game. As Steve recalls, "The store was a small, white-block building and it faced the boulevard, so you couldn't see the kids coming. I had absolutely no idea they were coming." When he realized the nature of the impending onslaught, Steve stationed some of the students around the store in order to stave off any would-be shoplifters. But he never really stood a chance. Before he knew it, the store was overrun with rambunctious teenagers. "After they left," Steve remembers, "there were actually half-gallons of ice cream lying in nearby yards. The kids would reach into the open air dairy case, grab the goods, and walk right out the door." Within minutes, he recalls, "They had cleaned me out. It was unbelievable." As Bob remembers, "Steve was there all by himself, and suddenly we've got 100 to 200 kids in a store that is only 600 or 700 square feet at the most! And Steve, he's going crazy, and he says, 'I don't know what the hell to do!' Finally, he just locked the door so no more could get in. He got walloped!"

As Steve remembers, the Pleasant Valley Boulevard location did not fare as well as the original store in terms of profitability. "But the rent was cheap," Steve points out. "It was 100 bucks a month, so we had one employee. We never had two people working full-time in this store during that period." The Pleasant Valley Sheetz Kwik Shopper employed a manager who worked six days a week, along with part-time help like Steve and his other siblings. Never content to rest on his laurels, Bob added new innovations to widen his customer base. As Steve observes, "We knew the lunch breaks at A&P, Butterick, and Veeder Root. We had a panel truck to serve lunch at the car shops in Hollidaysburg. We had sandwiches and chocolate milk," Steve adds. "We had a tricycle with an ice cream cooler. It was hard to pedal, but we filled it with novelties and would go to A&P to sell ice cream bars and popsicles for their afternoon breaks."

As the decade wore on and Bob contemplated opening up additional locations, the Sheetz family found itself at the mercy of fate, which dealt a double blow. On December 31, 1965, J.E. Harshbarger died of natural causes at 83 years old. Only a few months earlier, Steve had accompanied his grandfather to W.F. Sellers' Jewelry, where J.E.—always impeccably dressed in a suit and tie—purchased a Longines watch for his grandson in commemoration of his recent graduation from Altoona Area High School. For Steve's part, he wore the watch for the next three decades, never forgetting the day that his grandfather drove up in his black 1952 Chevrolet, grinding the engine's gears as they made their way to W.F. Sellers' Jewelry in the spring of 1965.

By the mid-1960s, Jerry's health had also begun to wane. Plagued since his 30s with diabetes, Jerry found that his "energy, his health in general, just all started to fade," Bob remembers. On February 23, 1968, Jerry died. He was only 57 years old. It was, not surprisingly, a terrible blow for his family. As Jerry's youngest son Louie recalls, "Our dad was a very warm person. Just a nice guy. He enjoyed immensely doing things with us: going to a ball game, taking us on summer vacations, and going to the Atlantic City boardwalk. He lived for that. Every night we would follow the same routine: we'd walk with him along the boardwalk and share a bag of peanuts."

Before he died, Jerry told Bob, "You know how to run a business," paying him the highest compliment that any son could hope to receive from his father, a successful businessman in his own right. As Bob mourned Jerry's untimely death, he realized that he had made a very conscious decision to remain on the career track that he had taken back in November 1952. He had chosen to follow a markedly different path from the dairy roots that he had established during his early days as his grandfather and father's youthful apprentice. And as the 1960s came to a close, he looked increasingly to his younger brother Steve to augment the family business that would make their name.

Bob Sheetz is pictured here as a young entrepreneur.

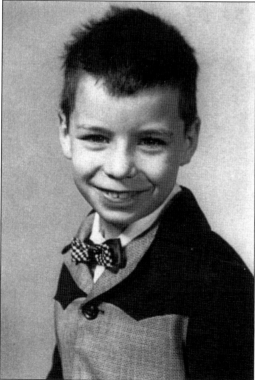

This early photograph shows Steve Sheetz.

"Shake a hand, make a friend" was an early advertisement for Sheetz Kwik Shopper, promoting the store's friendly, customer-oriented atmosphere. (Photograph by Kenneth Womack.)

J.E. Harshbarger is relaxing in Brigantine, New Jersey, just north of Atlantic City, his favorite vacation spot.

J.E. and Jennie Harshbarger are seen in their later years.

At a Rotary Club meeting are, from left to right, J.E. Harshbarger, Dr. Laurence Jones, and Robert E. Eiche, the director of the Altoona Undergraduate Center (later Penn State Altoona). Invited to visit Altoona by Harshbarger and Eiche, Jones was the much-revered founder and president of the Piney Woods Country Life School in Mississippi as well as a central historical figure in the educational advancement of African American students in the South.

Five

DUELING VENDORS, PUMPING GAS

In 1968, Bob Sheetz—remaining true to his vision of building a chain of convenience stores—opened up a third Sheetz Kwik Shopper. His brother Steve served as manager of the store, which was located on Hollidaysburg's Blair Street, one of the town's main thoroughfares. As it happens, the only real competition for the third Sheetz Kwik Shopper was a nearby A&P. Determined to ensure his new location's success, Bob strolled into the A&P on a Sunday and bought all of the store's bread, which he proceeded to restock on the shelves of the Hollidaysburg Kwik Shopper. Needing bread for their Sunday meals, the A&P customers made their way to Bob's store in short order. In this way, Bob succeeded in shifting customers' buying habits in his direction. He later accomplished the same end by buying out all of the A&P's Sunday stock of the *Pittsburgh Press*.

For Steve, a full-time management position at a convenience store during his senior year at Penn State University may have seemed like an unlikely choice—especially given his original career plans. Steve began his college career in January 1966 at Penn State's Altoona campus, where he enrolled as a full-time student for $130 per trimester in hopes of embarking upon an eventual career as a math teacher. As Steve remembers, "I liked math, although I didn't really know what I wanted to do. The only thing I knew for sure is that I liked math, and I loved numbers. It was all about numbers, so I decided I might as well go and become a math teacher."

As it happens, Steve's Penn State career began rather inauspiciously, with Steve flunking six out of his first 10 college credits. When his first report card was mailed home, Steve quietly intercepted it before it fell into his parents' hands. Meanwhile, with the military draft in play and the Vietnam War raging overseas, Steve knew that he had better improve his studies—and quickly at that. As he began enrolling in the math courses associated with his major, his grades started to improve, slowly but surely. At the time, Steve was still putting in a 25-hour week at the Pleasant Valley Boulevard location. One weekend, as Steve and his older brother took in a Pirates games at Forbes Field in Pittsburgh, Bob turned to him and asked, "Why don't you switch to business?" After transferring to the University Park campus, Steve saw the wisdom in his brother's advice and changed his major to management at the beginning of his junior year. Quite suddenly, Steve found that he "liked the business courses a lot better, because now we're really talking numbers!" Moreover, Steve recalls, "I loved statistics." And to his surprise, he found that he "loved psychology, too. I had to take 12 credits for my major, but I ended up taking 18 because I enjoyed it so much!"

As it turns out, Steve's intellectual renaissance could not have come at a better time. As he continued to make progress in his newfound major at Penn State, Bob asked Steve to consider a career with Sheetz Kwik Shopper. Steve demurred at first, telling his brother, "I don't know if I want to." But Bob, all confidence and ever true to form, simply would not take no for an answer. "Come on," he told Steve, "We're going to open 10 stores," even though he only had two locations at the time. "We're going to open 10 stores," Bob told him, "and you and I will both make a nice living." Thinking back on the exchange, Steve realized that he had been moved by Bob's ambition. "That's what convinced me," Steve recalls, "the idea that we would open 10 stores."

Steve's life had become further complicated—happily, that is—by a chance meeting with Nancy McCormick, a 1967 graduate of Altoona Area High School. Steve was working in the Pleasant Valley Boulevard store one evening in 1968 when Nancy stopped in to buy a pickle. As Steve recalls, "We had this barrel of pickles, and we sold a lot of them. One Friday night, Nancy came in—I think we may have run into each other in high school; she was two years behind me, but I didn't really know her." Steve asked her out on the spot. At the time, Nancy worked at Bell Telephone in Altoona. She remembers the evening like it was yesterday. That night, she recalls, "The girls and I were out riding around in one of their cars. Trying to find boys, probably. You know how it was back then. But we went into the Sheetz store and Steve was working. I went in to buy a dill pickle." Steve was funny, she remembers, and "he was a really nice person. But mostly he was very funny." Within a year, the couple married, with Steve later joking that "Nancy came in for a pickle, but got me instead!" But Nancy tells it differently. "That's not true!" she says. "I didn't even get the dill pickle!"

In December 1969, Steve graduated from Penn State, having married Nancy the previous June. He even interviewed with a few companies—Proctor and Gamble, among them—although he knew that he would most likely join Bob's business. Soon, Steve and Nancy had a budding family of their own, with daughter Megan born in July 1970, followed by another daughter, Nikki, in November 1971. Steve began his post-college career at Sheetz Kwik Shopper, where he made $150 a week as supervisor of the company's stores. And Bob could not have been happier with the new arrangement. "Working with Steve," he recalls, "we never had a harsh word. It was smooth sailing."

Shortly after Steve graduated from Penn State, Bob opened up the fourth Sheetz Kwik Shopper location—at the corner of Sixteenth Street and Washington Avenue in Altoona. For Bob and Steve, the new store was a landmark moment, given that it was the first location that they built from the ground up, rather than refurbishing a preexisting business. The new store's location was a triangular parking lot near the city's downtown Jewish temple, from which Bob purchased the real estate for $7,000.

For Bob, the Washington Avenue location afforded him the opportunity to maximize the store's layout to accent the finer points of his retail offer. "I knew we were making more money from the delicatessen items than anything else," Bob notes, "so it was the key feature when you walked into the store. When you walked through the front door, the first thing on your left was the checkout counter, the cashier. But then you saw the eight-foot delicatessen case. That's where we were making our money, selling lunch meats, selling chipped ham." Having positioned his sales leader front and center, Bob's layout drew customers into the store, not only providing him with the traffic that his business depended on, but also with the opportunity to sell at least one more item, and hopefully more, to ensure his profit margin.

In short order, Bob and Steve opened three more Sheetz Kwik Shoppers—located in Altoona's Juniata neighborhood, on Altoona's Howard Avenue (near the Altoona Hospital), and on Sixth Avenue and Fifty-seventh Street—bringing their total to seven stores. With Bob scouting out real estate, Steve took on the role of supervising the existing locations. Yet the Sheetz brothers' accelerated growth came at a cost—especially in terms of ensuring the cash flow that they desperately needed to maintain inventory across their chain of stores. The brothers needed cash—and they needed it in a hurry.

To accomplish this, they decided to replace their cash-on-delivery approach for paying vendors to monthly invoices. The Sheetz brothers devised this plan after attending a National Association of Convenience Stores meeting in Philadelphia and networking with other small business owners. In December 1971, they sent a letter to all of the Sheetz Kwik Shopper vendors announcing their new policy, effective January 1, 1972. To their surprise, very few of the chain's vendors took issue with the billing change. Bob and Steve even succeeded in prodding their vendors into paying for store shelving space and providing the first order for free. "Whoa, Bob!" an ecstatic Steve reported to his brother. "We have cash!" Flush with money, the brothers would open an astounding seven stores between May and November, doubling the size of their chain in the bargain. "We were so excited we found this cash," Steve recalls. "This is all we needed. In our mind, we thought 'we know everything there is to know about this business.' It was unbelievable!" And as history would demonstrate—if only temporarily—maybe it was.

For the balance of the year, the Sheetz brothers opened up store after store. "The new locations are coming like boom, boom, boom!" Steve recalls, "and I'm running everywhere. I'm in Huntington. I'm in Johnstown. I'm in State College. I'm in Altoona." But while the Sheetz brothers learned a variety of important lessons that year, Bob's yen for expansion never ebbed. His vision never faltered. On June 30, 1972, as they cut the red ribbon in front of their 10th Sheetz Kwik Shopper, a smiling Bob turned to Steve and announced, "Brother, let's open 100!"

And that is when the money got tight. Driving his Pontiac Parisian station wagon all across the region, Steve found himself at his wit's end trying to manage the swiftly growing convenience store chain. "Now comes September," Steve remembers, "and our business is really slowing down because kids are back at school. By October, I hadn't paid the August bills yet." Worse yet, Steve adds, "The last three, four stores we opened were just total dogs. So I have the vendors calling me now. Pepsi, Coke, everybody wants to be paid. Our cash flow is suddenly very tight. And that's when we went to our friendly neighborhood banker, John Beyer."

As Bob and Steve made their way to Mid-State Bank in downtown Altoona, they hatched a plan. "You are going to be the bad guy today," Bob told his younger brother. "You're going to be the fresh young college kid. I know John, and I'll tell him that everything was okay until you came along and wanted to really push the growth. We'll get things straightened out." As Steve remembers, their plan disintegrated almost as soon as John entered the room. "He's really beating up on us," Steve recalls. " 'I told you guys,' John says. 'You're growing too fast. You ought to listen to me, and here you are begging for cash.' " Beyer took the Sheetz brothers to task, forcing them to take control of their business. "You guys don't even know how much money you make!" he exclaimed. "You have got to start taking inventory; you'll get an inventory crew. You'll get a controller. You're going to get an accounts payable department. You're not going to open a store for a year!' " Directing his fury at Bob, Beyer remarked, "I wish we had a set of blinders we could put on him so he could never see another potential store location!"

As Steve recalls, at that point in the meeting, Bob suddenly looks at his brother, then turns to their banker, ready to receive his onslaught yet again: "John, I've already signed four locations, and we're going to start paying rent. I'm going to be paying rent whether the stores are open or not. We're going to have to have cash flow." Although he was livid by this point, Beyer loaned the Sheetz brothers the money that they needed to make ends meet but not without first ensuring that they would hire a person to assemble an inventory crew. "Her name was Sandy Bice," Steve remembers. "I had to beg her to join us. She was with J.C. Penney, doing inventory, when she came on board. And she did a great job. Suddenly, we began to know how much money we were making, how much we were losing with theft, and so forth." Beyer also insisted that Bob and Steve hire a controller.

Looking back, Steve recalls that "1972 was a really difficult year. The vendors were just hounding us to death for money. But we learned a number of lessons. We had been taking essentially short-term money and buying long-term assets. Bob and I went into that year thinking, 'All we need is cash, and we're going to make this thing run.' But it was much more complicated than that."

Now that Bob and Steve had a bona fide chain of convenience stores on their hands, they were eager to think more expansively about their industry. For quite some time, Bob had been keenly aware of the Sheetz Kwik Shopper's regional competition—stores like the Country Garden Market and Leighty's Farm Market, to name two. But Bob began to consider the industry from a much larger perspective after seeing a plaque for the National Association of Convenience Stores in a 7-Eleven store. "Who's successful?" Bob wondered. "And what are they doing to improve their offer?" What they were doing—as Bob learned at yet another National Association of Convenience Stores meeting—was offering self-serve gasoline. And with the repeal of the blue laws in Pennsylvania greatly diminishing Sheetz Kwik Shopper's profit margins, Bob and Steve needed a news sales leader to drive their business.

As fate would have it, the Commonwealth of Pennsylvania had approved self-service gasoline sales in December 1971. During the National Association of Convenience Stores conference, Steve met a representative for Autotronics, a firm out of Houston, Texas, that specialized in installing gas tanks for service stations. The Autotronics rep promised Steve that his company would install the gasoline station apparatus—including the installation of the tanks and other equipment—for free, provided that his firm could split the profits with the Sheetz brothers. In truth, Steve admits, "We knew nothing about gasoline." But the idea of expanding their offer and adding a sales leader like gasoline—and for free, no less—was too much to pass up. With Autotronics doing the heavy lifting, Bob and Steve began offering gasoline sales in 1973 at their eighth store, a location at Sixth Avenue and Lloyd Street in Altoona that had opened back in May 1972. The building used to house an old pizza shop, Bob recalls, until its owner fell on hard times. "The reason it closed up," Bob remembers, "was that it was owned by a bookie. He was probably the biggest gambler in town, and this was where he was running all his cash through. They had a raid in Altoona one day on all of the pool rooms and gambling places. They caught him, and they locked him up. He was out of business. And that's where we came in!" As the first Sheetz Kwik Shopper to offer gasoline sales, it was a landmark moment in the history of the company.

As it turns out, the city of Altoona was no stranger to milestones in the petroleum industry. In 1909, Reighard's gas station opened up in the city, cementing its claim as the oldest existing gas station in the United States. Yet the Sheetz Kwik Shopper—with its convenience store offerings in addition to gasoline sales—was a markedly different proposition, providing its owners with a diversity of profit-making sales points. For Bob and Steve, the arrangement with Autotronics became stale rather quickly. As Bob notes, their agreement involved a "collector's program," in which Sheetz Kwik Shopper acted as the collector. As Bob explains it, Autotronics "came in, dug the hole, buried the tanks, and set up the device beside your cash register to authorize the pumps." This left the Sheetz brothers to collect the sales dollars and split the profits with the company from Houston. The collector's program allowed Autotronics to set the daily price for gasoline because they bore the original costs for the inventory, the equipment, and its maintenance. "It was a collector's program," Bob notes, "because we had to deposit all of the money in their bank account at four o'clock every afternoon. Whatever we sold the previous 24 hours had to be deposited in their account. The plan was that we were to split the profits, but Autotronics said we never made a profit."

After their experience with Autotronics, Bob and Steve were confident that they could do better. "After that first store with gasoline," says Bob, "we knew we had to find better partners." Having soured on the experience of working with Autotronics, Bob and Steve opted instead to work with a series of jobbers and national brands in order to try and learn the gas business. It was an arduous process for them, to say the least. The Sheetz brothers would wait until 1976 to open their first store expressly offering the Sheetz brand of gasoline.

Kathleen Sheetz, age 61, is seen here in January 1973.

This latter-day photograph shows J.E. Harshbarger.

Steve and Nancy Sheetz are pictured here in the early 1980s.

Six

"LIKE SPOKES ON A WHEEL"

"I always knew Bob wanted 100 stores," says Steve, thinking back on the early 1970s. "Ten was just a stepping stone." While they continued to nurse their ambition for expanding their chain of convenience stores, the Sheetz brothers were still smarting from their meeting with John Beyer about their business practices. "We were humbled for a little bit," Steve recalls. "Bob learned how much he didn't know about site location, that he was really going to have to work at getting better. For the first few stores, he was only picking one a year. For a while there, we thought we were magical; just open up a store and they will come."

For his own part, Steve knew that he had to make some much-needed changes in terms of his approach to supervising the brothers' growing number of locations. "I realized that I needed to change my ways," Steve observes. "I was so tight in terms of money that I wouldn't dare hire someone until we were ready to open a new store. I learned that we needed to put a much higher value on people, and we had to think about creating a training program." Worse yet, says Steve, "going into 1972, we didn't have a single office person, not one staff person besides Bob and me. My schedule at the time involved driving from store to store and doing the checkouts, making out bank deposits, and making grocery orders."

Steve recognized that he was not trusting his store managers to do their jobs—even down to the level of pricing goods for sale. "Why was I like that?" he asks, looking back. "Because I didn't trust you to do that. A manager at a Sheetz Kwik Shopper was just a figurehead at that point. I would let them interview potential employees, but I had to approve every person, and I also made out each store's schedule. Essentially, I didn't delegate a thing because I didn't trust anybody, and that would lead to really huge problems by the end of the year." In short, Steve realized that he needed to reevaluate his entire approach to the business, echoing Beyer's cautionary words to the Sheetz brothers. "I had to go back to square one," he recalls. "We had to start all over again. By early 1973, we were starting to stabilize, but we had four stores coming online. In the space of a single year, we had doubled our size, which was absolutely nuts."

In addition to following Beyer's advice and adding inventory teams, Bob and Steve also came to recognize that they could not open up another store under their one-sided arrangement with Autotronics. As the Sheetz brothers continued to navigate the newfangled world of retail self-service gasoline, Sun Oil Company approached them about a partnership, and Bob and Steve ended up leasing several of their existing gas stations in cities like Indiana, Pennsylvania, as well as Johnstown and Blairsville. Ultimately, says Steve, "we learned that we had to begin to do installations on our own." As a test case, Bob and Steve installed the gasoline apparatus at their new location near Penn State University's Altoona campus. "I'm thinking cheap again,"

Steve recalls. "The whole installation is $7,900 for the tanks, two little pumps, and no canopy. I remember thinking at the time, 'Why would I put in a canopy?' It doesn't rain that much anyway!" After a problematic gas pumping system prompted Bob and Steve to end their arrangement with Sun Oil, they turned their attention to Gulf, which provided them with a branding opportunity by providing free credit card services for Sheetz Kwik Shopper customers.

After a massive marketing campaign in order to sign their customers up for Gulf credit cards, the company's new CEO ended the free credit card opportunity, and the Sheetz brothers learned an invaluable lesson that would resonate well into the present day. "We learned that branding in a subsidiary relationship is not going to work for us," says Steve. "We have to retain control, and we don't want to exist at the whims of a new CEO because there will always be new CEOs. It's the nature of the beast. We made the decision that we're only going to sell Sheetz-brand gasoline and control our own destiny." The brothers' decision to protect themselves and their customers by having their own brand had far-reaching consequences for the future of the company. In many ways, it was the defining moment as they charted the future of the Sheetz Kwik Shopper.

But the road to self-branding was not always easy. After the Sheetz brothers signaled to other retailers in the region that they were in the gasoline business to stay, service station operators rallied against the newcomers. During those early years, the service stations denounced Sheetz Kwik Shopper, often claiming that the Sheetz brothers stocked subpar gasoline—a great irony, because the service stations and Sheetz Kwik Shopper stores were serviced by the very same pipelines and, quite often, the same tanker trucks. As Steve remembers, "The service operators hated us taking their business. So, now, if you ever had a problem with your car, the first question the service-station attendant would ask would be, 'Where do you buy your gas?' 'Sheetz.' 'Well, that's the problem,' the attendant would answer. 'They sell crappy gas; they put water in the gas.' " With their 38th store, located on Twenty-fifth Avenue in Altoona, the Sheetz brothers drew a line in the sand. They would weather the storm in favor of self-branding. It would define their stores, once and for all, from top to bottom. But they knew the risks. As Steve points out, "Once we made the decision to go out on our own, now we're really subject to these gas station operators telling our customers, anytime they had an automotive problem, that 'you're buying that shit gas.' "

For all of the challenges that accompanied their forays into the gas business, there is little doubt about the power of self-serve gasoline as their new sales leader. It transformed their business and allowed them to continue opening up new locations at a steady pace. By the mid-1970s, Sheetz Kwik Shopper began standardizing coffee sales throughout the chain, further diversifying the company's offer. It was indeed a period of great change. As with Steve, who learned how to trust his managers and delegate his expanding duties, Bob made a number of strategic changes of his own. By this point, he was in charge of negotiating with lenders and scouting out new site locations. But in contrast with their early years, when Bob amassed new locations by retrofitting other businesses, he began working directly with contractors to build future stores from the ground up. As with their new philosophy about gas installation, they had decided to take matters into their own hands when it came to construction. "We reached a point where every building was a new building," says Bob. "We weren't buying old ones. We started to build from the ground up as early as 1977." As Steve recalls, after the Johnstown flood occurred in July of that year, the cost of building out the company's stores nearly doubled from $48,000 to $94,000. "That's when we began to construct our own buildings," says Steve. "We formed our own construction crews," Bob adds, "and we still have our own crews in operation today."

Bob also continued to refine his approach to site selection, being increasingly careful not to pit his stores in close competition with one another. He would draw concentric circles out from their Altoona hub in order to plot out new locations farther and farther away from the center. "Like spokes on a wheel," Bob recalls. The Sheetz brothers' efforts to revamp their business in the wake of Beyer's scathing remarks also led to the welcome rehabilitation of their credit outlook. "We were making money now, and the banks were good to us," says Bob. "I went in, I had a whole plan of what I was focused on, what I was going to try to accomplish, and I was making my payments on time. I was what the bank wanted: a young entrepreneur."

During the 1970s, Bob and Steve stimulated the chain's entrepreneurial spirit at every turn. To accomplish this, the brothers rolled out hot dog offerings at all Kwik Shopper locations. At first, sales were sluggish, with most locations averaging around 100 hot dogs sold per week. In order to promote greater sales, Steve held wiener incentive contests to pit Kwik Shopper locations against each other in company-wide competitions with the goal of selling more than 1,000 hot dogs at each store per week. In many ways, the Kwik Shopper hot dog offerings were a precursor to the company-wide food promotions that would transform the company in the late 1980s.

In order to alter the company's business practices even further, Bob instituted an advisory board in 1976. In so doing, he tempered his yen for expansion with a concerted effort to hone the company's vision for the future. By this point, says Bob, "my vision was redefined in an effort to create orderly expansion. Now, I took my time selecting sites. With this new philosophy and with regular planning meetings, we opened as many stores as we could as long as I thought they were in the right location and would be successful."

Within a few years, Bob brought his young brother Joe onto the Sheetz Kwik Shopper team. Joe had served for many years as the general manager of the J.E. Harshbarger Dairy Company. In 1980, the eldest Sheetz brother Jim sold the dairy to Galliker's, a Johnstown-based dairy company. Bob and Steve briefly considered buying the J.E. Harshbarger Dairy Company for sentimental reasons. As Steve remembers, "Bob thought it would be nice to keep the Harshbarger name going and that we could run the dairy. At that point in time, we had just come through some unbelievable growth, and we were probably up to 75 or 80 stores by then, and we had our hands full. I said, 'If we buy the dairy, first of all we're going have to make a whole new investment because we all know that the dairy is antiquated. That means we're going to have to take money from the stores. Second, I don't have the core competency for running that dairy. I would have to learn that and, quite honestly, I don't see any advantage because we're at the point, with 80 stores, that we can negotiate a great deal on milk.' There was really nothing to be gained."

After Galliker's purchased the dairy, Joe spent the following two years transitioning the company into its new ownership. In the process, the J.E. Harshbarger Dairy Company's seven-decade history came to a close. But the company's legacy—now, arguably, alive and well in the ever-expanding chain of Sheetz Kwik Shopper convenience stores—was still in its relative infancy. With the sale of the J.E. Harshbarger Dairy Company, Joe welcomed the opportunity to join Bob and Steve at the Sheetz Kwik Shopper. With Joe in the company's fold, Bob decided to diversify his approach to site location by teaching his younger brother how to scout out real estate. As Bob remembers, "Joe rode with me three days a week as we scouted out locations. In no time, he was getting pretty good at picking sites and we started to see dividends. In one year alone, he located 19 new sites—and some of them were very good." As Joe's son Joe Jr. (born December 2, 1966) notes, "My dad came from the dairy, where his experience was operations. And suddenly he shifted from being general manager of a dairy to real estate, which he had zero experience in, but learned from Bob. My dad loved real estate, so it was a big deal in his mind when Bob said, 'That's what I want you to work on' because he knew that was one of Bob's big focuses. Bob attempted to teach him everything he knew about real estate in a very short period of time and, of course, dad took it and ran with it." And did he ever. As his daughter Ashley (born March 18, 1989) remembers, "Dad was constantly out at intersections, counting cars, looking at places to build. When we were little, we thought that it was crazy that we could say 'Where's store number 279?' and he could give you the exact intersection, the town, everything. It was amazing!"

As Joe's younger son Travis (born May 24, 1970) recalls, the addition of Joe to the Sheetz Kwik Shopper management team in the early 1980s shifted the company's chemistry in new directions. As Travis notes, "Dad was different in many ways from Steve and Bob. He had a great work ethic—as they do certainly—but he wasn't driven in the same ways. For dad, it was more about the process than it was about the end goal. He was very well respected around the company. He didn't speak a lot, but when he did, everyone was like, 'Joe's talking.' Steve always called him the 'voice of reason.' When we'd get crazy with our thinking, my dad was the one who would always bring them back to earth."

In 1979, Bob and Steve's brother Charlie also left the J.E. Harshbarger Dairy Company, where he served as plant manager, to join Sheetz Kwik Shopper. He had worked for several years at the dairy after graduating from Slippery Rock University with a degree in elementary education and a specialization in math and science. For Charlie, life at the dairy had grown stale—"I didn't like the job anymore," he recalls. "It just wasn't me any longer"—and working with his brothers afforded him with a chance to try his hand at a new career path involving the company's array of food offerings. For Louie, the youngest Sheetz brother, working with Bob and Steve was hardly a foregone conclusion. Louie graduated with an accounting degree from the Indiana University of Pennsylvania with every intention of finding employment in his chosen field. But then Bob came around—as he so often did with especially talented prospects—and coaxed Louie into joining the company. "Why don't you come work for me?" Bob asked. "It was an offer I couldn't resist," Louie recalls. "I could tell that it was a new generation, that Bob and Steve were eyeing a new era of professionalism."

For Bob, the company's success throughout the 1970s—and poised, as it was, for even greater opportunities in the 1980s—was inextricably associated with gasoline sales. "It was Steve," Bob remembers. "Gasoline was all Steve's idea. That's probably the number one part of our success story because of the profit margin in gasoline over the years, how we developed and refined it further, how it works as a sales leader and builds traffic for our offering inside the store." Gasoline had truly emerged as a proven sales leader that allowed the company to greatly improve its margin. Not long afterwards, Bob's dream of opening 100 stores finally came into being with the gala debut of a new location in the Greenwood section of Altoona in 1983.

Without question, gas sales now functioned as a key element in Bob's tried-and-true formula for convenience store success. "We're always trying to sell our customers just one more item. You've already paid the rent with the first item. Get one more item and your overall gross margin dollar percentage at the end of any year runs between 31 and 31 and three-quarters percent. In one of our best years, we had 32 and three-quarters percent. Now, imagine," Bob adds, "just imagine if we do a billion and a half dollars in overall sales and can get one more percentage point on a billion and a half. Just get one more percent. At that scale, one more percent is $15 million in additional profit." Given the company's humble origins with the Sheetz Dairy Store, it was astounding simply to imagine such financial heights. But as usual, Sheetz was only just getting started.

As Sheetz Kwik Shopper continued to grow, Bob and Steve Sheetz supplemented their deli products with a selection of doughnuts and other baked goods. This photograph was taken in store No. 15 in Tyrone, Pennsylvania.

The deli case in Sheetz Kwik Shopper No. 40, in Mount Union, Pennsylvania, is pictured here.

By the mid-1970s, coffee had become a best-selling staple in Sheetz Kwik Shopper locations.

In 1976, Bob Sheetz established the company's first advisory board. This 1979 photograph shows an early incarnation of the group. From left to right are (first row) Bob and Steve Sheetz; (second row) Irv Bregman, Bill Ward, Lucius Kellam, and John Hudgins.

With the sale of the J.E. Harshbarger Dairy Company to Galliker's in 1980, Joe Sheetz (pictured) welcomed the opportunity to join his brothers Bob and Steve on the Sheetz Kwik Shopper's management team as a site locator.

In 1979, Charlie Sheetz (pictured) left the J.E. Harshbarger Dairy Company and joined Sheetz Kwik Shopper to help shape the company's growing array of food offerings.

Louie Sheetz, the youngest Sheetz brother, graduated from the Indiana University of Pennsylvania, joined Kwik Sheetz Shopper, and provided the company with new marketing and product strategies.

Seven

"ANYTHING THEY CAN DO, WE CAN DO BETTER"

By the advent of the 1980s, the Sheetz brothers had transitioned nearly all of their convenience stores to 24-hour operations, and gasoline had become the proven sales leader to draw customers into Sheetz Kwik Shopper locations. But as Bob's son Stan notes, gas sales in the early 1980s were a far cry from contemporary standards. "We put two pumps in," says Stan. "Typical installation was two pumps and no canopy. It was not big gasoline thinking by any stretch of the imagination." While big-time gasoline strategy might not have been the norm at this time, the days of self-serve gasoline service had come to stay. As Stan points out, over a 20-year period, the United States "went from some 250,000 gas stations to 150,000; at the same time, convenience stores went from selling fewer than 10 percent of the gallons sold in America to over 80 percent of the gallons sold. It took over 20 years, but by retail standards that is lightning fast to witness such a business upheaval."

Flush with their ever-growing yen for expansion, Bob and Steve tried their hand during this period at creating different franchises in an effort to complement their evolving Sheetz Kwik Shopper offer. As Bob notes, these additions were practical choices as much as they were efforts to improve their profit margins. As Bob remembers, "We got to the point where we didn't want competition beside us. They might take our parking." But as Earl Springer, manager of Employee Programs, adds, sideline restaurant franchises also afforded the Sheetz brothers the opportunity to add beer sales to their offer, since it was legal to sell beer in Pennsylvania in restaurant settings. "The whole concept was more than just trumping the competition," says Earl. "It was to get the beer licenses and open up a new sales leader."

The first of these franchise innovations was known as the Sandwich Saloon, a deli-style sandwich joint complete with Old West–style doors. As Charlie recalls, "I worked in a Sandwich Saloon in Hollidaysburg in August 1980, when I joined Bob and Steve. Next door was a Sheetz Kwik Shopper with a couple of gas pumps out front. By 1982, I ended up managing all of the Sandwich Saloons." Next up was Chicken Charlie's, which was fashioned after Kentucky Fried Chicken's offer. "The character of Chicken Charlie, complete with a mustache, was modeled after me," says Charlie. "The Chicken Charlie's locations started out doing very well when they opened. We had four of those, including locations in Altoona, the Oakland section of Pittsburgh, Punxsutawney, and Washington, Pennsylvania. Eventually, we added Mr. Donut franchises and a Häagen-Dazs ice cream shop, which we operated for a year."

With the Sandwich Saloon and Chicken Charlie's restaurants under his supervision, Charlie emerged as the manager of the Sheetz brothers' early forays into retail food sales. In short order, the company abdicated some of its sideline franchises. As Charlie observes, "Dunkin' Donuts was expanding, and Mr. Donut was weak competition, so we got out of the doughnut business. And Häagen-Dazs, which we opened near the University of Pittsburgh, was just a dumb idea. It was an experiment, but really, when you think about it, the best time for ice cream is spring and summer, but that's when the students go home! So 90 percent of the kids are gone and that's when you sell ice cream. And meanwhile, it's not a real good thing to have a Häagen-Dazs store in the middle of winter. So that didn't work. That was one of our trial-and-error mistakes."

As it happens, the company's Sandwich Saloon and Chicken Charlie's franchises ultimately proved to be lackluster elements in terms of boosting the overall Sheetz offer. But as with the company's 1970s-era attempt at diversifying its offer by supplementing convenience stores with laundries, the sideline restaurants afforded Bob and Steve invaluable retail experience. "We had two laundries, and they were a headache," Bob recalls. "And we lost our shirt on them. But everything you lose on like that, you gain something from it. There's some experience there." As Stan points out, experiences like these—even though they fail to become permanent elements of the overall company offer—are always valuable. "Anything they can do, we can do better," says Stan. "We'll take them for a while and we'll study them, but we're not keeping them." Looking back, adds Steve, "we got into trouble in the 1980s when we got away from our focus on convenience stores. Working to get back to our strength, we closed the sideline restaurants and sold 15 Pittsburgh locations that didn't fit our model."

For this reason, Sheetz Kwik Shopper was consciously re-branded in 1982 as Sheetz—just Sheetz—the name by which most of the company's customers already knew their neighborhood convenience store. As the Sheetz brothers slowly retreated from franchise innovations such as the Sandwich Saloon and Chicken Charlie's, the Sheetz offer began to stabilize around standard convenience fare such as soft drinks, dairy products, and snack items. As Louie observes, "This was a high point for the Pepsis, Cokes, and Mountain Dews of the world. They were booming. Bottled juice was here for the first time. The dairy-packaged tea was a big item, as were the individual portions of milk. Proliferation of more snack brands, candy, chips, that's where our business was coming from. We still did a decent business with milk and bread. Deli was still there on some level," he adds. "We were still holding onto it, but it wasn't a big revenue generator anymore."

And as Stan points out, the company had an entirely different problem altogether. When he joined Sheetz in the early 1980s, he was charged with bringing the company's financial department into the late 20th century. As Stan recalls, "One of my projects was to bring the accounting and reporting up to date. We had to get a computer. We had to get things computerized. Because we're growing. We're 85, 90 stores, and we're still writing stuff on paper ledgers. It was a little bit painful, to say the least." At this time, Stan brought his well-honed financial background into play. As with so many of his relatives, Stan had cut his teeth working for the family business. After earning a masters of business administration from Pace University and serving a stint practicing high finance in New York City, he proudly joined Bob and Steve back in Altoona. In addition to updating the company's technology, Stan remembers, "I started working on restructuring the entire balance sheet because we were still dealing with Mid-State Bank. We brought in Fidelity Bank from Philadelphia to share the risk because we were beginning to become a very large client."

Manning the financial helm for the Sheetz brothers, Stan discovered that the company was mired in a weak position. "We were borrowing at prime plus 2 percent," says Stan. "Whatever the outstanding loan was, we had to have 10 percent of that sitting in a checking account. Sitting there, doing nothing. So we're only borrowing 90 percent of our money and paying prime plus two for it. So I went shopping." After outgrowing Mid-State Bank's lending capabilities, Stan shopped for a new deal beyond Altoona. At first, Bob and Steve contacted a trio of Pittsburgh-area banks—PNC, Mellon, and Equibank—on the advice of John Beyer. To their surprise, all three banks passed on the opportunity to work with Sheetz, citing the company's spotty credit picture as their reasoning. "It wasn't real easy, Stan recalls, "but we were a growing company. We had a good reputation. We were attractive, I think, too. Finally, Philadelphia National Bank was the one that I brought in, and they were great. I gave them a sales pitch on a Thursday and the following Monday, they called and said everything's approved as requested." In one fell swoop, Stan had completely reconfigured the company's credit outlook. "We completely restructured all of the company's debt," says Stan. "The new deal allowed us to borrow and get capital at a reasonable rate."

As it turns out, Stan's financial wizardry could not have come at a better time. After some 32 years as the prime force behind Sheetz, Bob had decided to enjoy a well-deserved retirement in Boca Raton, Florida, in 1984. But to nearly everyone's surprise, Bob announced in the fall of 1986 that he had more than mere retirement in mind—he wanted to sell his controlling interest in the company. As Ray Ryan, longtime company man and executive vice president for purchasing, manufacturing, and distribution, remembers, "It wasn't even announced at the time that Bob was going to sell. It was that Steve was taking over and running the business." Even Stan was surprised, later recalling that his father called him in September 1986 and proclaimed that he wanted to sell his controlling interest in Sheetz; at the time, he held a 90-percent stake in the company. As Stan remembers, "This was not the phone call I was expecting! I'm suddenly having a bad hair day here!" Not missing a beat, Stan countered by saying, "Will you give Steve and me the chance to buy the company?" Bob agreed to sell them his interest, but with one proviso: "Oh, by the way," he told Stan, "you have to buy the company by December 31st because that's when capital gain taxes go up."

Stan sprung into action. "Three months to get it done," he remembers thinking. "Okay, fine, we'll get it done. We went through all the motions, what we had to do. I hired and fired an investment banker because he wanted equity—he wanted a piece of the deal." The transaction required to recapitalize Sheetz was both remarkably simple and enormously complicated at the same time. On the one hand, notes Stan, "Bob owned 90 percent of the company, and Steve owned 10." Carrying out a necessary appraisal of the company's assets gave his father pause, Stan observes. Realizing the economic effect of a total buyout, Bob settled back into his well-honed gambler's persona—and in so doing, made it easier for his relatives to consummate the deal. "My father was very gracious," Stan recalls, "and let's remember he has an appetite for risk—which is why he is great—and he took back half of the purchase price in a subordinated note, which really helped make the financing possible." After being concluded in record time, the recapitalization that afforded Bob's buyout still came with a significant cost. "The family and I borrowed $3.6 million to buy out Bob," says Stan. "In truth, we also bought $33 million in debt and, as we very soon discovered, a rapidly declining business."

Bob's retirement capped a whirlwind seven years in which the company dramatically shifted—and then re-entrenched—its retail offer, redefined its financial practices and drastically modified its credit outlook, and continued its furious pace of growth and expansion. Yet for Steve, it ushered in a new era of uncertainty and concern. "When Bob left, he took the vision with him," Steve lamented as he considered the company's future without Bob in the captain's seat. But as Steve soon discovered—and happily at that—he had more than a few tricks left up his sleeve.

Bob's son Stan Sheetz, pictured at left with his father, joined the company in the early 1980s after earning a masters of business administration from Pace University and serving a stint practicing high finance in New York City.

A new store opening shows Steve and Bob Sheetz with Altoona mayor Allan G. Hancock and Hope Eckenrode (far right), regional director of operations.

In 1982, Stan Sheetz announced the company's change of name from Sheetz Kwik Shopper to Sheetz. Kathleen and Bob Sheetz are pictured on the left, with Phil Schreyer, vice president of Human Relations, and Jill Shaffer, Miss Pennsylvania 1981, on the right.

Bob Sheetz unveils the company's new logo, along with the new Sheetz tagline, "We keep on changing for you."

The company's new logo and color scheme would remain in vogue for more than two decades. Steve Pellegrini of Blair Sign Company designed the first Sheetz sign. Over the years, Blair Sign Company has built all of the Sheetz signs and gas canopies.

Bob and Steve Sheetz celebrate the company's re-branding as Sheetz—just Sheetz—with commemorative ball caps.

Bob Sheetz is pictured with Pop Sheetz, the company's mascot during the 1980s.

A Pop Sheetz advertising display for the company's inflation-proof hot dogs and "Pop's Large" soda-fountain drinks is pictured here.

The Pop Sheetz mascot participates in a 1980s store opening.

Pop Sheetz welcomes customers at a former Sheetz location in downtown Pittsburgh, at Liberty Avenue and Ninth Street.

Pictured here is a Pop Sheetz commemorative key chain. (Photograph by Kenneth Womack.)

Stacks of egg cartons are seen at Sheetz store No. 40, located in Mount Union, Pennsylvania, during the company's "pile it high—watch it fly" era.

This fully stocked grocery aisle is in the newly re-branded Sheetz location in Mount Union, Pennsylvania.

Store No. 204 in Murrysville, Pennsylvania, was the first Sheetz location to offer 16 fueling positions. At the time of this photograph, it was the number one Sheetz gas pumping location in terms of overall sales.

Eight

Total Customer Focus, 24/7

Looking back, Steve describes the mid-1980s as the company's "lost years." And they were indeed a turbulent time, to say the least. But the company that emerged in the new decade was certainly much different—and in nearly every possible way—than any of the Sheetz managerial team could have remotely imagined.

The real culprit in the company's unrest, as it turned out, had precious little to do with restaurant misfires like the Sandwich Saloon and Chicken Charlie's, or with its history of expansion, or with Bob's recapitalization. Rather, it was the express result of severe demographic changes that were, slowly but surely, depleting the company's business and placing the future of Sheetz at risk. American social and economic life had been shifting, and the Sheetz team, like so many businesses, had been late in recognizing this new world order.

First, America's tradition of home-cooked meals had been replaced by "casual dining." Today, the Applebee's restaurant chain serves no fewer than two million customers per day. This is a far cry from the 1970s and early 1980s, when families still prepared and consumed their meals at home together. In 1984, a total of 72 percent of America's meals were homemade. By 2007, that number had dropped to 57 percent. "All the growth of the restaurant industry has been about takeouts," according to industry expert Harry Balzer. "It's making your life easier to eat at the place where you really want to eat anyhow, which is your home." Second, these shifts that Balzer and others describe correspond with dramatic changes in American economic life, which moved from families with single breadwinners to both spouses making a living in the workplace, not to mention single-parent families and other variations.

Not surprisingly, the boom in US restaurant culture mirrors these shifts, with Americans having fewer and fewer hours to devote to buying groceries and preparing home-cooked meals. The numbers truly speak for themselves: according to the National Restaurant Association, restaurant revenues in 1984 topped out at $164 billion. By the second decade of the new century, that figure exploded to over $600 billion. When the Sheetz managerial team began to analyze these changes, they were startled to discover that not only had their retail offer not accounted for such shifts, it had actually gone against the grain of US eating habits. As Steve points out, "If you study the percentage of meals eaten at home versus the percentage eaten away from home, you'll see how rapidly these changes occurred—but not just in the 1980s. It was in the 1970s as well." Worse yet, says Steve, "we realized that our model hadn't changed for 20 years. We kept putting the same model out there while people's lifestyles changed very quickly. Literally, these people—our customers—were moving further and further away from us."

Looking back, the changes that Sheetz had established over the years were small gestures—and occasionally counterintuitive—to the growth of America's restaurant and takeout culture. "We had made tweaks in the model," says Steve, "like in 1975, when we added coffee. We went 24 hours, but the basic model hadn't changed. We still had deli offerings." But as Steve notes, Sheetz's deli space actually decreased during this period of expansion in the takeout and take-home food industry. When Bob started back in the 1950s, the company devoted considerable space and effort to its deli offering. As Steve points out, "It started out as a 10-foot deli, then we moved to an eight-foot deli, then a six-foot deli, then finally to a four-foot deli. Our reaction to the deli business going away—to these changes in the industry—was to make the deli smaller. What are we doing? We're shrinking it, but we weren't really adding any new revenue sources." And the chain's overall foot traffic was beginning to reflect this increasingly glaring dilemma. "By 1987, Sheetz was in trouble," says Bob. "Customer counts were decreasing. We are in possession of a stagnant model. One of the key statistics we keep track of is customer counts—especially customer counts per store. And these numbers were dropping fast. The customers were going to our competitors because, flat-out, they were doing a better job than we were."

In the wake of Bob's retirement and the company's recapitalization—and with even greater shifts in America's eating culture seemingly on the horizon—Steve recognized that Sheetz needed to make wholesale changes of its own in order to survive and compete in this new retail world. And these changes needed to happen with all deliberate speed. "The world was changing quickly with people eating out more and more," Steve recalls. "In the 1980s, we had a take-home model, but what we really needed was an immediate consumption model."

As it happens, changes in the Sheetz offer had been warranted for quite some time. By the 1980s, the retail mix at the company's nearly 150 stores was haphazard at best. As Dave "Woody" Woodley, vice president for Development and Product Sales, observes, "From an entrepreneurial perspective, it was a very spirited time." On the positive side of the balance sheet, store managers were given free rein to build up their product offering. On the other hand, such a diversity of operational styles and offerings diluted the overall nature of the Sheetz brand. During the early 1980s, Woody managed the company's Patton, Pennsylvania, location. As Woody recalls, "I created my own things. On Thursdays, I sold hot sausage from the grill. I sold hamburgers from a hot table. I made my own sauce—ketchup and Pepsi for ribs. The business was very decentralized during that period. I dealt with my own suppliers. I had local candy guys that'd come in, and I negotiated my own deals and set my own specials." During the holidays, says Woody, "I built racks outside of the store and sold Christmas trees out of the parking lot. I raffled live turkeys for Thanksgiving." As Joe Jr. remembers, "Everybody did their own thing. Store managers would make a Crock-Pot full of Sloppy Joes at home—or brownies or whatever—and sell them in the store the next day."

In addition to the wide disparity in store offerings, there were also ongoing issues with the Sheetz grocery profile. Some years back, the company experimented with enhancing its grocery store product line. The seventh store, located on Sixth Avenue in Altoona's Eldorado section, was built out at 15,000 square feet—much larger than the standard 2,000-square-foot store at the time—in order to accommodate the grocery line. As Steve recalls, the location had "produce, deli, and a lot of grocery. We were going to use the produce to get more into the grocery business and the deli business. It was a much bigger store, and a much bigger operation." In retrospect, says Steve, "we did really well with fruit baskets; we did some catering, but my goodness, keeping the produce fresh—that was very difficult. In truth, we didn't really know the produce or the grocery business." Feeling that they had gone too far with a larger-scale grocery store, the company eventually repurposed the Sixth Avenue location as their corporate headquarters.

But some elements of the Sheetz grocery effort lingered on—namely, canned goods and other grocery fare. During this period, Earl Springer was managing the Williamsport, Maryland, location.

With grocery sales declining across the chain, he recalls being tasked with marking down canned goods in order to try and shore up the company's fading business. "We called it 'cutting the cost of convenience,' " Earl remembers. "This is when sales went flat and, for some reason, we thought that people really wanted to come in and buy cans of peas at Sheetz. We thought we were a mini grocery store so we lowered the price on cans of peas and stuff off the shelves. In truth," adds Earl, "there's no way that we could compete with a grocery store who's buying cases of green beans or ketchup. We went through everything. We went through every grocery item on the shelf and lowered the price on it, and it was such a big deal that management had to come in to oversee the change. We had to go through every item with a sticker gun, pull off the old stickers, because that was one of our policies—that you couldn't put a sticker over a sticker—take all the old stickers off, clean the can, and re-sticker it with the new price." It was an onerous process, to say the least, and the company's management quickly learned that the discount was not helping to improve their grocery sales.

And that was just the grocery line. In terms of its deli and food business, Sheetz was still dealing with a long-standing problem—one that had no easy answers. As Earl points out, "When I started with the company 30 years ago, nobody, but nobody, unless they were drunk and it was three o'clock in the morning, wanted to eat food from the same place that they purchased gasoline." The gas pumps out front were still providing the sales leader that Sheetz required, but the customer count—the in-store foot traffic—was becoming more and more difficult to generate. It was becoming increasingly challenging, to quote Bob's old adage, to sell that one additional item that made the profit margin possible. As Joyce Twombly, a former store manager and the company's learning specialist in the Leadership Development Department, notes, "We were still known for our delis. We would sell a lot of lunch meats and cheeses." But even that business—the company's bread and butter, in addition to cigarettes and gasoline—was drying up.

As if to compound matters, Steve was finding himself at his wit's end in terms of running the company's operations. He realized, for the first time, that Sheetz had developed into a rigidly autocratic organization. And since Bob had retired from day-to-day operations, that left Steve as the chief autocrat. "I really hadn't brought everyone in to help me run this business," says Steve. "If we were going to change things, then it was going to be about changing my management style. It was about changing my model as much as changing the store model. The organization, the culture, it had to change." After Bob's departure, Steve discovered that he had inherited a fairly large staff. "I had about 24 people reporting to me, which made me feel really good on the one hand, but I also came to learn that they weren't necessarily doing a good job, and I certainly wasn't developing them. I thought to myself, 'How can I improve the company with 24 people reporting to me?' "

The result, as Ray Ryan vividly recalls, was Steve's "March massacre." "We had dropping customer counts, low sales, increasing expenses that we could see at store level," says Ray. "Steve was feeling these pressures, and he had to change the direction of the organization. Somehow, we had to become more customer based instead of management based." When the March massacre ensued, Steve felt that his back was against the wall, that the company had reached its lowest ebb. "I distinctly remember the day it happened," says Ray. "It was a small conference room with all of the district managers sitting around the table. Steve walks in and announces, 'We're in trouble, and we've got to shake things up. I'm taking this company to the top with or without you, so you'd better be ready to change and do things differently.' Suddenly, everybody was just sitting around, literally quaking in their boots, wondering about how their worlds had just changed." In the meantime, Steve began remolding the company. A number of managerial reports were fired, while several administrative-level employees left the company.

According to Ray, a few weeks after the March massacre, Steve threw the district managers another curve ball. "Steve walks into the conference again," Ray recalls, "and this time he announces, 'I have an opportunity for everybody.' Remember," Ray points out, "he just told us we're in trouble, not good financially, no bonuses, that everything has got to change. And now he's saying, 'If you want to invest in the organization, I have an opportunity.' " All of the district managers sat around the table, Ray remembers, and nobody said a word. No one responded—except Ray. "It was a defining moment for me," he recollects. "I had no money, three children, a mortgage, and a new baby on the way. So I went to my wife and said, 'Do you think your dad will lend me some money?' And the next thing you know, I'm an investor in a company that owns Sheetz real estate. I have a vested interest in the future of the company." It was Ray's opportunity to go all in. "I'm looking at guys like Steve, who are daring to go to the top or fail trying. They're taking risks. Why wouldn't I take a risk, too?" As it turns out, Ray was the only one around the table who joined Steve as an investor in his bid to turn the company around.

Jim Wenner, the company's vice president of technology, describes Steve's personal transformation during this period as a shift from being a CEO-like authority figure to a much-needed motivational coach. With the Sheetz corporation, says Jim, "you have to remember that you're not working for a company that wants to be here today and gone tomorrow. They're not living for quarterly profits. They're not doing things simply for tomorrow, with tomorrow being the next month. They're going for the long term." For Steve, going for the long term meant not merely being his employees' coach, but a motivational figure on behalf of the company's customer base as well.

In addition to reshaping his managerial team, Steve also changed the company by being humble, by taking his hat in hand and going directly to the company's waning customer base to find out exactly where he and his colleagues had lost their way. He could not help remembering Bob's metaphor about the nadir of any convenience store: the lone hot dog slowly turning 'round and 'round on a greasy rolling grill. He believed that they had fallen that far and that it was high time that they transformed the nature of their offer, that Sheetz remake itself—and in radical ways, if necessary. "Our company had developed a culture of fear," says Steve, "our customer counts were falling, and we needed to revolutionize."

For Steve, the revolution began in Hagerstown, Maryland. "My brother Louie and I went to a Holiday Inn, where we met with 40 heavy users of Sheetz and 40 heavy users of our competitors. Louie and I spoke with each of them, one-on-one. It all boiled down to 'where do you shop and why?' What came out of those meetings was what customers wanted, which became our mission, and it's still our mission today. They wanted fast, friendly service, they wanted quality products, and they wanted clean and convenient locations. The other thing they wanted was for us to be open all the time. We were already open 24 hours, so we couldn't really do any better in that regard."

Through these focus groups, Steve and Louie learned that stores with concrete rather than blacktop pavements were judged to be cleaner, as were stores with as much outside lighting as possible. Meanwhile, stores with more windows were not only judged to be cleaner, but safer, too. Furthermore, as Steve remarks, "Customers want to be able to see open parking stalls from the street, as well as open gas pumps. That means more pumps and more parking. It means canopies in case of inclement weather. And on the food side, it means fresh, quality products." And in what turned out to be a master stroke, it also meant cleaner restroom facilities. The logic was simple but powerful: if customers can count on clean restrooms in every location, then it suggests that an operation that values cleanliness and safety should be able to deliver high-quality food and sell gasoline under the very same brand. It was revolutionary—so revolutionary, in fact, that Steve required that every restroom feature a prominently displayed vow of cleanliness, complete with a toll-free number to report any sanitary infractions directly to him.

"What we did," says Steve, "was become totally customer driven. We followed up the focus groups with surveys of 1,500 customers across our service area. We defined our new vision as Total Customer Focus, and we reorganized around a simple premise: to provide our customers with fast and friendly service and quality products in clean and convenient locations." It was decidedly simple, and, one way or another, it would be the founding of a new era for the company. Steve was going to go to the top all right—or fail trying.

After Bob became chairman in 1984, Steve Sheetz (pictured with daughters Nikki and Megan) succeeded his brother as the company's chief executive officer.

Over the years, the Sheetz company has repurposed its Sixth Avenue Altoona location, originally built to be a grocery store outlet, as the organization's corporate headquarters.

Sheetz company headquarters is pictured as it looks today at its Sixth Avenue location. (Photograph by Roseanna Shumskas.)

A commemorative key chain celebrating the opening of the company's 150th store in State College, Pennsylvania, is seen here. (Photograph by Kenneth Womack.)

By the mid-1980s, Sheetz was experiencing declining customer counts. Consumer complaints were centered on cleanliness, safety, and convenience. In an effort to understand growing customer dissatisfaction, the Sheetz brothers conducted consumer surveys among focus groups in order to reinvigorate their business. The result was the Total Customer Focus (TCF) program, which accentuates, in Steve's words, "fast and friendly service and quality products in clean and convenient locations."

The only time the Sheetz family is satisfied is when our customers are."

Stephen G. Sheetz
President

Quality
"We search for the finest quality products. We thoroughly test them internally and with customers before we roll them out chain wide."
Louie Sheetz
Vice President Marketing

Service
"Like our products, we look for the best employees. We train them. We motivate them. And we reward them. At Sheetz, the customer is everything."
Charlie Sheetz
Vice President Human Resources

Convenience
"We've introduced a new concept in store design. Our new stores are bright, spacious, and located in high traffic areas to make shopping easier, faster, and hassle free."
Joe Sheetz
Vice President Store Development

"Before we put our name on the sign, it all has to be right for the customer."
Stephen G. Sheetz
President

Customer Satisfaction
"We do everything we can to provide our customers with the finest, quality products at reasonable prices and we serve them fast, without compromise...24 hours a day, every day of the year."
Stan Sheetz
Vice President Operations

Sheetz
open 24 hours

As a result of the Total Customer Focus program's implementation, Sheetz revamped its locations, adding larger, more widely lit canopies.

Dave "Woody" Woodley, vice president for development and product sales, is seen here.

Pictured here is Ray Ryan, executive vice president for purchasing, manufacturing, and distribution.

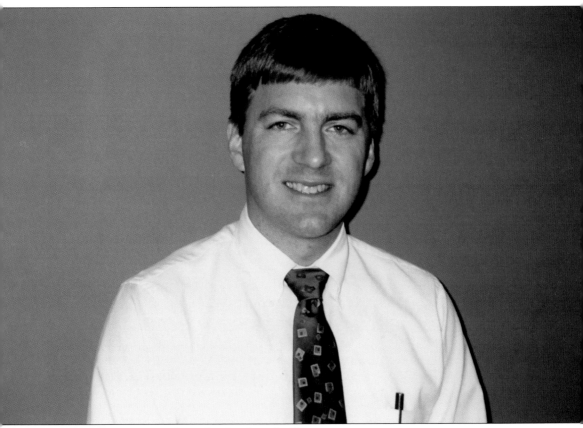

Jim Wenner is vice president of technology for Sheetz.

Nine

"I Want My MTO!"

In the late 1980s, as Sheetz was quite literally cleaning up its act as part of its Total Customer Focus vision, the company was delivered yet another godsend—and this time it came straight out of Williamsport, Maryland, fewer than 10 miles from where Steve and Louie had held their mission-changing focus groups only a short time before. At the time, store manager Earl Springer was struggling to promote the company's standard deli offer. His district manager, Dolly McCarty, was one of the company's great entrepreneurs in the days before the retail mix had been rendered consistent throughout the chain. As Earl remembers, "Dolly knew how to hustle stuff and make money. She would go up to Reading and buy stuff from the outlet malls to resell in our stores. One time, she bought giant piggy banks. She'd mark them up by 75 percent, but people would still buy them. She had an amazing eye for merchandise, and she really fit into the culture at the time."

But in spite of her entrepreneurial talents, Dolly was unable, like Earl, to succeed in the deli business. "Frankly," says Earl, "our Williamsport customers were used to going to places—large supermarkets—with a much larger selection. We just had a hard time competing in the deli market." In order to improve the Williamsport store's profit margin, the Sheetz managerial team selected it as a test location for a new fried chicken offer. It was an expensive proposition involving a $25,000 remodel in order to accommodate the chicken fryers. The company even hired a fried chicken expert from Louisiana in order to ensure the quality of the new offer, which they marketed as Yankee Fried Chicken. At first, the fried chicken offer succeeded. As Earl notes, "It sold great during the summer months, but when summer ended the sales just dropped." Steve was quick to notice the profit loss, remarking to Earl, "What is going on here? Your sales, your food service margin has gone to nothing!" Worse yet, the Yankee Fried Chicken offer required 20 minutes of preparation, with a short, 45-minute shelf life afterwards. "So we were constantly frying chicken and then throwing it out," Earl recalls. Once again, Steve was livid at the failure of the new offer. "What's going on?" he asked Earl. "Do you have a plan to straighten this out?"

As it turns out, Earl had a plan all right. With Yankee Fried Chicken on life support, he turned his attention back to the store's deli counter. "You know," he said to his staff, "our pre-made subs aren't selling because no one wants the stuff that was made 12 hours ago. Why don't we make subs to order? We have a deli, we have the stuff here, why don't we do this as a renegade program?" To bring his plan to fruition, Earl located a $1,100 sandwich-preparation unit. "Remember," says Earl, "this was in the days before Subway and Blimpie's had really made their mark." The idea of freshly made sandwiches was still fairly novel. At the time, the Williamsport store sold a paltry 96 pre-made subs per week, so Steve needed to be convinced about purchasing the prep unit. "You get $1,100 and not a penny more!" he told Earl.

In a covert marketing-research effort, Dolly and Earl went to area sub shops and bought several different varieties of sandwiches. "We brought them back to my store," says Earl, "and we took the subs apart, and we weighed how much meat was on them and how much cheese was on them." Dolly and Earl's goal was to make their sandwiches larger than the competition's, albeit with a slightly higher price point. Ultimately, they came up with six different sandwich varieties, including Italian, ham and cheese, turkey, tuna, chicken, and roast beef. With recipes in hand, Earl trained his staff to make the sandwiches consistently. For his customers, Earl printed order sheets that were placed atop the deli counter.

In its inaugural week, Earl's new sandwich offer seemed like a bust. "In the first few days," Earl recalls, "we sold fewer freshly made sandwiches than we did pre-made subs, so I'm thinking 'I'm out of here. Steve's going to tell me to pack my bags.' But the thing was, I had neglected to market the idea." With nothing to lose, Earl and his staff put a sign in the window, "Come Inside for Fresh Subs." At the same time, they placed cutout footsteps leading into the store entrance. Each footstep was labeled with the words, "Follow Me to Made to Order Subs." To Earl's surprise, "All of a sudden, people started saying, 'Wow! Made to Order? So you guys now make subs to order?'" After launching an advertising campaign on a local country music radio station, the Williamsport store's freshly made sub sales doubled. Within no time, they were averaging 350 sandwich sales per week, easily outclassing their pre-made sub numbers. Quite suddenly, the Made to Order sandwich phenomenon was born. With sales finally on the uptick, Steve asked Earl to share his idea with the nearby Taneytown, Maryland, location. Unveiled on May 1, 1986, the Taneytown location was the first new store to open with Made to Order food.

As a marketing entity, Made to Order received a shot in the arm a few years later when Jeff Wild, the company's director of food service at the time, was driving to work from Johnstown to Altoona. He found himself trailing a cable television truck with the words "I Want My MTV" on one side and "HBO" on the other. In a moment of epiphany, Jeff merged the cable truck's verbiage with the Made to Order concept, coming up with a marketing blitz behind the phrase "I Want My MTO." With Jeff's clever promotions angle, the abbreviated MTO took off as a sales phenomenon in its own right. As Earl points out, "Made to Order made a lot of sense. By telling customers that something is 'made to order,' you're letting them know that they can have anything that they want on the sandwich. More importantly, we're not going to charge you extra if you don't want lettuce or if you want tomatoes. It's not à la carte, where you are subject to an upcharge." Not surprisingly, before long, MTO was exported to all the stores in the Sheetz chain.

By the early 1990s, MTO had become a genuine sales leader in its own right. And with Total Customer Focus still in its infancy, these newfangled concepts were a marriage made in heaven. The notion of freshly made sandwiches perfectly complemented the new mission, which connoted fast, friendly service and quality products in a clean and convenient location. For Sheetz, MTO was the game changer that the convenience store chain sorely needed in order to expand its customer base. And did it ever. As Steve points out, "MTO was a home run. Not only did we sell sandwiches, but we came to recognize that the size of our sales basket increased because the MTO became the centerpiece of a meal; when you bought an MTO, you inevitably needed a drink and most likely you also needed a bag of chips, pretzels, a fruit cup, what have you. Because it was a driver for other products, the MTO increased our gross margin across the board." As the company rolled MTO out across its convenience stores, sales began jumping by as much as 15 to 20 percent.

While MTO proved to be a revelation for the company, the same could not be said for the MTO order forms that Earl originally devised back in Williamsport. As Joyce Twombly recalls, Earl's form led to a tablet with tear-off sheets. "We had these little golf pencils," she recalls, "and you would write on your order what you wanted—lettuce, tomatoes, onions. Then you would place your sheet in a basket on top of the sandwich unit. It was an ineffective setup because customers learned pretty quickly that they could game the system by putting their sheet on the bottom, which is where the oldest orders were located. Sometimes, it caused a stir—especially at lunchtime."

Determined to create an alternative to the MTO tear-off sheets, Stan discovered the solution at a National Association of Convenience Store conference when he met a pair of technology entrepreneurs from Radiant Systems who were exhibiting a touch-screen demo. Stan realized that their system could spell the welcome end for the already antiquated tear-off sheets, which had become expensive in their own right. As Stan points out, "Anytime we wanted to change the menu, we had to reprint MTO order forms for every single store." Worse yet, Stan notes, "the tear-off sheets required customers to write—and any illegibility creates inaccurate orders." With touch-screen technology that relies on pictures, Stan adds, "customers can see what they're ordering, while also creating a time-stamp for their transaction." After testing out a prototype in the Greenwood location in 1994, says Stan, "we discovered that customers not only embraced the touch screen; they loved it. MTO sales immediately went up by 12 percent."

As Daniel "Chef Dan" Coffin, director of culinary development, observed, the rise of MTO also afforded Sheetz with a means for creating a consistent food product across the chain. In short, it provided another means through which the company could standardize its brand. As Chef Dan points out, "With an MTO, we don't necessarily cook—we let the vendors do the cooking in advance. When employees prepare an MTO, they are really working at assembling it correctly and consistently before it lands in the customer's hands. When the ingredients arrive from our vendors, tomatoes are pre-sliced, lettuce pre-shredded, and so on. This frees our employees from having to establish a competency in slicing and shredding. Rather than building those competencies, we'd prefer that they'd build the competency of providing customers with a consistent and well-assembled product."

In this fashion—by becoming a sales leader that spurred the success of other products and helped standardize the company's offer—MTO was a truly galvanizing force for Sheetz. Like the Total Customer Focus vision, it was a consolidator that solidified the very same company brand that, only a few short years before, had been flagging. But as Steve notes, "After Total Customer Focus and MTO, we had a whole new problem. It was a good problem to have, but a problem just the same." In order to bring the twin visions of Total Customer Focus and MTO into being, the company had to remodel its stores considerably. "When we realize that MTO is a winner," says Steve, "we're going to roll it out across the company. What goes behind that roll out is unbelievable because we have to double the number of employees in order to have enough staff to meet the demand. When we asked customers what they wanted back in the late 1980s, they said that they wanted fast, friendly service, quality products, and clean and convenient locations. When we asked employees what they wanted in the workplace, they wanted to work with somebody else. With MTO, that was a necessity. So it all kind of fits together. We're building a model that the customer wants and that the employees want, and it requires more labor. But it also requires an entirely different store design and layout." The shift in the company's personnel requirements was dramatic. In the early days, Sheetz stores sported a handful of employees. Today, the average Sheetz location employs 32 people. By transforming the company's approach to staffing its locations, Total Customer Focus led to an employee-centered model—one that underscored the significant role that the company's staffers play in building and maintaining their customer base. As Stan points out, "We know we're doing well when our employees are happier clocking in than clocking out."

As it turns out, ground zero for the twin installation of the Total Customer Focus and MTO vision was the company's 158th location in Lewistown, Pennsylvania. But as Steve points out, the company's new era required an entirely new store. "In response to the focus groups," says Steve, "we're going to build a facility with a canopy and lots of lights. Customers are going to feel safe here, with more windows, larger and cleaner restrooms. We're going to triple the pumps from two to six. It's going to be more inviting, with more and better-trained employees. But I know that, with all things being equal and the gas price being the same, the customer is coming to Sheetz. If we've got a superior facility and superior employees, Sheetz wins."

"It sounds simple," says Steve, "but, of course, it's not that simple. The new store in Lewistown sits on an acre and a half footprint. Up until then, most of our stores occupied a half-acre, maybe three quarters. So we've got a new and better model that meets our needs with Total Customer Focus and MTO. Unfortunately, we now have about 150 stores that don't fit the model and only one that does. This makes for a heavy capital need," Steve adds, "because we're going to dramatically increase the number of labor hours along with the number of employees. We're also going to have to rebuild or remodel 150 suddenly antiquated locations."

Although the company indeed found itself confronted with the enormous capital expense of a mammoth redesign, the silver linings were equally impressive. Looking for a new sales leader to complement the company's burgeoning food and gasoline sales, Louie began experimenting with a new product line of inexpensive cigarettes in the 1990s. Known as Jacks, the Sheetz cigarette brand with its distinctive Jack of Spades packaging provided customers with a lower-priced alternative to premium brands, which accounted for the majority of cigarette sales at the time. With the big supermarket chains, Louie notes, "you throw a carton of cigarettes in the cart along with everything else and take it home for the week. It was rare that people bought a single pack at the supermarket, so that's what we sold, single packs. But we said, 'What if we sold our packs for a really cheap price?'" As Louie explains, "What was happening was the cigarette companies were taking these ridiculous cost increases. They were milking that business right under our eyes because they saw consumption dropping in the face of increased health awareness. They said, 'This game isn't going to last forever. Let's harvest, let's make what we can.' So they started taking ridiculous price increases." Seeing an opportunity to create a new marketing niche, Louie devised a promotional scheme in which Sheetz offered customers much better value than the prevailing price of $1.40 per pack. "Let's sell them at a dollar," Louie told his brothers. "Let's see if we can't make some noise."

And did they ever. As Louie points out, "We weren't selling single packs below our cost, but if we were selling them at $1.40, let's say we used to make 60 cents a pack. Now we're making 15 cents a pack." By giving up 45¢ per pack of cigarettes, the Sheetz brothers consciously chose not to make the money that they formerly earned on cigarette sales. "But a funny thing happened," says Louie. "Sandwiches were up, drinks were up, candy bars were up. The discounted cigarettes were bringing in foot traffic, and customers were buying other products. Suddenly, our customers realized we were a value play, with our great price on cigarettes and gas." For that time, Louie concludes, "it was the most organized, effective marketing we did. We were getting noticed because we had great prices."

Louie's new marketing strategies were indeed a coup—and they ran counter to contemporary notions about convenience stores, which suggested that customers were willing to pay higher prices at outlets like 7-Eleven in order to enjoy the convenience of 24-hour purchasing opportunities and alternative, closer proximities than their neighborhood supermarkets. The boom in cigarette sales also mirrored the overall success of the company's Total Customer Focus strategy.

As Stan observes, Total Customer Focus and MTO changed virtually everything because "they altered the business volume per store." Sheetz was now benefitting from the remarkable convergence of its new mission and the MTO model, Stan notes, "and then Louie comes up with the brainchild of lowering the price of cigarettes as far down as it can go, and suddenly cigarette volume triples." With sales leaders like MTO and cigarettes in place, Stan reports, "we went three years in a row where sales-per-store increased by more than 20 percent. That's unheard of for a retail chain. That's just absolutely unheard of, but that was the growth that we experienced in the early 1990s." The company was firing on every cylinder—and with all three of its sales leaders in top form. Amazingly, says Stan, "gas volume went way up, MTO volume went way up, and tobacco volume went way up. It was just incredible."

Perhaps even more impressively, Steve found himself working from a decidedly different perspective as the 20th century came to a close. What seemingly began as all-out disaster in the late 1980s—and in the years since Bob's retirement from day-to-day operations, no less—had rebounded in truly remarkable and innovative ways. But it had hardly happened by accident. By leading the company in a concerted effort to redouble its attempt to become customer centered and responsive to vital cultural and demographic shifts, Steve and his team had given the brand new life. As the successes associated with Total Customer Focus and MTO so resoundingly demonstrate, Steve had truly righted the company's ship.

In the late 1980s, Earl Springer created a new sandwich offer at the Sheetz location in Williamsburg, Maryland. To advertise the new product, Earl and his staff put a sign in the window, "Come Inside for Fresh Subs." At the same time, they placed cutout footsteps leading into the store entrance. Each footstep was labeled with the words, "Follow Me to Made to Order Subs." To Earl's surprise, "All of a sudden, people started saying, 'Wow! Made to Order? So you guys now make subs to order?'"

Here, Steve Sheetz is making an MTO. For Steve, the MTO—as with the Total Customer Focus program—was transformative, challenging the company to reimagine its way of doing business.

Pictured are Stan Sheetz (right) and his uncle Joe. The company's MTO sandwich line found its marketing niche after Jeff Wild, the company's director of food service at the time, coined the slogan, "I Want My MTO."

With the incredible success of MTO, Sheetz revamped its locations to support the sandwich line.

A blizzard of direct-mail and in-store promotional pieces—nearly all with a coupon offer and complete menus and prices on the reverse—helped Sheetz customers overcome any lingering doubts about MTO quality and value. Similar "grass roots" blitzes are planned for new MTO hot sandwich and salad programs.

As with Total Customer Focus, MTO was rolled out across the Sheetz convenience store chain, eventually moving beyond sandwiches and deli fare to encompass a wide array of food items, including salads, pizza, and breakfast items, among others.

93

Processing MTO food orders was automated through the use of touch-screen technology. In this photograph, Sherry Hancock, manager of training, explores the first generation of Sheetz touch screens with an employee.

A later version of Sheetz's touch-screen ordering system is seen here.

Pictured is a contemporary version of Sheetz's touch-screen ordering system.

Earl Springer is pictured here in later years with Dan McMahon, executive vice president of operations.

Over the years, Sheetz has promoted a number of in-house brands, including Jacks cigarettes, It! Cola, and Spudderz potato chips (pictured).

Sheetz also introduced Nova Blue, its house brand of bottled water.

Ten

ALTOONA, WE HAVE A PROBLEM

The history of Sheetz is marked by moments of risk—of key instances associated with Bob's well-known gambler's persona and Steve daring to remake the company. But their greatest risk, the moment in which they would go the farthest out on the proverbial limb, was still in the offing. It was a moment in which the Sheetz company defied contemporary expectations—and, however briefly, the advice of their own legal counsel and public relations firm—to, plainly and simply, do the right thing.

As it happens, events transpired so quickly that the Sheetz management team scarcely had time to fully recognize how fluid the situation really was. As Steve recalls, "We were at the annual Calgary Stampede. Nancy and I were traveling in Canada with friends. I got an urgent call from Phil Freeman, our director of human resources at the time, and he said, 'There's been a Salmonella outbreak. We don't know that it's Sheetz, the Pennsylvania State Department of Agriculture doesn't know that it's Sheetz, but they do know that a couple people who have eaten at Sheetz have gotten sick.' And that was late Monday afternoon; on Tuesday morning, I was headed back. We called a meeting of our executive team for that afternoon at one o'clock." When Steve called the meeting to order back in Altoona, with Stan participating by phone, it was Tuesday, July 13, 2004.

What Steve did not know at the time was that the Pennsylvania Department of Health had registered several reported salmonella infections in the state during the previous week. By Friday, July 9, the department's health lab identified at least 12 *Salmonella javiana* cases across four states: Pennsylvania, Ohio, Maryland, and West Virginia. As part of its protocol, the department alerted the Centers for Disease Control and Prevention that an apparent food-borne salmonella outbreak was in progress. Later that same day, case-patient interviews identified the food source as deli items purchased from Sheetz locations in Pennsylvania and Ohio during the past 72 hours. The patients had consumed lettuce and tomato products prepared for Made to Order sandwiches, wraps, and salads.

During the previous week, the company preemptively ordered the removal of all produce with an expiration date of July 12 from its locations across the chain, which was comprised of more than 300 stores at the time. Sheetz also proactively alerted the company's produce supplier, Coronet Foods out of Wheeling, West Virginia, about the reported salmonella contaminations. At the same time, the Sheetz corporation began working with the US Food and Drug Administration to begin tracking the history of the recent infections in order to quarantine the outbreak.

Sitting in the conference room with his executive team the next afternoon, Steve was all but certain about how he wanted to frame the company's crisis-management plan. He and Stan were in full agreement about how they would work to resolve the issue. As Steve remembers, "We had our public relations people in there, of course, along with our chief counsel. On the one hand, you've got the PR people wondering 'What's the right thing to say?' while the lawyers are being overly cautious, saying 'We've got to be careful with the liability side of this.' So I am sitting here in the meeting," says Steve, "listening to all of the counsel, which is what you should do. But by late Tuesday afternoon, I informed the team that 'it's pretty obvious that this is our problem here.' "

"Remember," Steve points out, "at that point, they didn't even know what it was. They didn't know for sure if it was a tomato or if it was lettuce. They thought it was lettuce at the time. So we had the attorneys telling us, 'Don't come out with anything yet.' The PR people are still strategizing about how to frame the situation. But Stan and I knew what we had to do. We had to stay with our vision—to live or die by it. We kept coming back to Total Customer Focus, which is our pledge to our customers. I'm thinking to myself," Steve adds, "that if I'm the customer I would say, 'I want to know, Mr. Sheetz, what do you know and what don't you know, right now?' They may be telling you from the PR side 'Don't say anything' with the lawyers saying 'Definitely don't admit anything,' but, in the end, if we're totally customer focused, the customer wants and deserves to know the truth. So we told the executive team, 'We really think that we need to go on TV tonight.' "

That evening, Steve held a press conference to offer a no-holds-barred explanation of everything the management team knew at that moment. He was well aware of near-doomsday scenarios that disease outbreaks can spell for restaurant chains, with stories about Jack in the Box's E. coli contamination and Chi-Chi's hepatitis crisis still fresh in the industry folklore. But he and Stan were determined to wager the company's future on the vision that had served as the catalyst for its resurgence. To Steve's mind, Total Customer Focus was not merely a retail-sales mission; it was a contract between the Sheetz company and its customers to look out for their welfare at all costs. As he readied himself for the press conference, Steve remembers, "We now know that there are 125 people sick, confirmed. Sixty of them have eaten at Sheetz. We don't know if it's lettuce, tomato—we don't know what it is, but we know with a high correlation that the people had eaten at Sheetz." Meanwhile, knowing that the company would receive an avalanche of telephone calls after the press conference, the Sheetz management team set up a dedicated call center.

The press conference was held at the Sheetz training center, not far from the company's Altoona headquarters. With just three hours' lead time, numerous news outlets, both broadcast and print, were on site, with others linking in via the company's live feed. During the press conference, Steve was honest, frank, and decidedly transparent about the company's state of affairs. "We have a problem," he announced. "We don't know exactly what it is, but we have a problem. And that's what we know so far, and what we're here to tell you is we're going to take care of it. If you're sick and you seek medical help, we're going to pay. If you have to take time off from work, we're going to take care of you." Just as Steve predicted, the press conference produced a flood of calls. As Steve recalls, "It was like boom! Those phones absolutely lit up."

The following day, Wednesday, July 14, the Pennsylvania Department of Health formally announced that a salmonella outbreak associated with food prepared at Sheetz convenience stores was under investigation. At the same time, the Pennsylvania Department of Health and the Centers for Disease Control and Prevention began a coordinated investigation of the outbreak. By this point, Pennsylvania, West Virginia, Maryland, and Ohio had reported some 56 cases of salmonellosis in connection with food purchased from Sheetz stores. By Friday, July 16, Coronet Foods publicly acknowledged that it had provided sliced Roma tomatoes to Sheetz stores. Not long afterwards, the Pennsylvania Department of Health confirmed that salmonella had been discovered in an unopened bag of sliced Roma tomatoes prepared by Coronet Foods and obtained from a Sheetz store in Greencastle, Pennsylvania. By August 6, the Pennsylvania Department of

Health confirmed that 330 cases of salmonellosis had occurred in Pennsylvania, along with more than 80 cases in neighboring states. Most of the cases were associated with the consumption of Roma tomatoes in Made to Order food products.

For Sheetz, the fallout was swift and dramatic. Wasting little time in order to protect its customers' welfare, the company destroyed all of the produce that had been in the same batch as the infected tomatoes. But even their concerted effort to quarantine the contaminated produce could not stave off the inevitable. As Steve remembers, "We watched our sales just plummet. In the coming weeks and months, our food sales fell by 40 percent, but interestingly enough, the customer counts were not dropping as rapidly. People were still using us, but they were buying a bag of chips or crackers or something prepackaged. We were shocked by how much the sales dropped, but the customer counts didn't really drop that much." Yet even as sales fell, Sheetz refused to allow its employees to pay the price. Employee hours were never decreased during the downturn.

To Steve's mind, the stability of the customer counts demonstrated that Total Customer Focus was working, that their basic vision was sound. "I think the Total Customer Focus is one of the key philosophies we have," says Steve, "which is that this business is run for the long term. We're not making short-term decisions here. When I was at Penn State, if there's one thing I remember, it's that business is an ongoing concern. You can't make short-term decisions; it just doesn't serve you well. Total Customer Focus," Steve points out, "is about taking care of the customer, and if you don't make any money this month or lose money for a year, then that's what it's about. Total Customer Focus makes everything crystal clear. If your attorney says that the outbreak is going to cost us $10 million, then I say, 'alright, then, $10 million.' If I were to lie to a customer and lose that customer's trust, then I lose the business; what's that worth? I'm not going to risk that customer's trust for any amount of money. Whatever it costs—$20 million, whatever—we're going to take the hit because it's about doing the right thing. It's Total Customer Focus, after all, not Total Profit Focus."

As Stephanie Doliveira, vice president for human relations, remembers, "The outbreak got very serious, very quickly. I would say what impressed me the most was the integrity of the family, always wanting to do the right thing. It blew me away. People *want* to work for companies like this. I think the average person wants to work for a very good company, but it's not until you see the leaders of your company in a situation like this that you realize, 'Wow. This is an amazing family. This is an amazing organization. They really truly want to do the right thing.' And ultimately, they did." As it happens, even the attorneys were impressed. William Marler, the Seattle-based lawyer who represented 60 of the victims from the salmonella contamination, lauded Sheetz for its swift efforts to protect its customers, especially in terms of compensating victims as well as paying for medical bills and lost wages associated with the food-borne illness. "They're not only doing the responsible thing," Marler exclaimed. "They're showing that businesses really do care about their customers' well-being, and not just the bottom line." The July 25, 2004, issue of *Business Journal Daily* praised Sheetz for its handling of the crisis, writing that "fast action by the company, and well-timed public-relations initiatives, prevented the Salmonella outbreak from becoming a public-relations disaster." The same article also quoted Steve, who refused to concern himself with public relations tactics, remarking that "We have said all along that our absolute priority is to ensure the safety and well-being of our customers and employees."

Echoing Steve's inspired, customer-centered message, Stan dedicated himself to identifying the supply-chain issues that allowed the contamination to occur in the first place. "We have to do right by our customers," says Stan. "If you're not moved by the stories of our customers' suffering, then nothing makes you feel bad. There was the couple who ate subs at our store before going on their honeymoon, when they came down with Salmonella from an MTO. There's the guy on vacation who just had a kidney transplant and now, all of a sudden, he comes down with Salmonella and he's in the hospital because he's taking anti-rejection drugs and he's been contaminated by Salmonella from our food products. Fortunately, nobody died. You've got older people, you've got younger people. You've got anyone whose immune system may be compromised. Salmonella normally won't kill you, but it can."

In an effort to track down the source and nature of the contamination, Stan and his team isolated the trucking routes that delivered the contaminated Roma tomatoes from the farm to Coronet Foods and eventually the Sheetz Distribution Center. As it turns out, says Stan, "the contaminated tomatoes were all processed together. They were all shipped together to stores across our chain. Going forward," he adds, "we learned an enormous amount of information from the Salmonella outbreak. We learned where we had weaknesses in our system and we fixed them. We've learned now how to deal with vendors, our suppliers who could potentially provide us with contaminated product. We've set policies in place. For instance, we will not handle raw protein in our distribution chain. Won't happen. We'll handle raw produce, but we will not handle raw protein and, if we're going to handle raw produce, we're going to find out who we're buying it from and we're going to do random inspections at their facilities; we're also going to demand to review our vendors' inspection reports, all of their scientific testing, on a regular basis."

In this fashion, the salmonella outbreak prompted Sheetz to redouble its efforts to prevent such contaminations in the future and to protect its customers' welfare. Looking back, as Steve has noted, the company's salmonella crisis was far more than a public relations or legal challenge. It was an opportunity to witness, firsthand and with very real implications, the power of Total Customer Focus working on behalf of the vast Sheetz customer base, to recognize the basic humanity that was invested in Sheetz's fundamental vision. In many ways, it was the company's finest moment.

In October 1995, Stan Sheetz (pictured on the cover of the July 2006 issue of *Chain Store Age*) succeeded his uncle Steve as the chief executive officer of Sheetz.

In 1994 and 1995, Sheetz was ranked "Convenience Store of the Year" by the National Association of Convenience Stores (now the Association for Convenience and Fuel Retailing).

Stephanie Doliveira, pictured here, is vice president of human relations.

Eleven

"PUTTING OURSELVES OUT OF BUSINESS"

The story of Sheetz, as Steve himself points out, is a quintessentially American story. It is a story about taking risks on behalf of an idea, about painstakingly working to refine that idea, about pursuing innovation in the face of ever-changing cultural and demographic shifts. And, as the salmonella outbreak so clearly demonstrates, it is also about doing the right thing no matter what the short- or long-term economic risks may be.

As the 21st century moves into its second decade, the Sheetz corporation has been rewarded—and handsomely, at that—both for remaining true to its carefully defined vision and for becoming one of the industry's most respected leaders and innovators. Since the advent of Total Customer Focus and MTO in the late 1980s and early 1990s, the company has enjoyed widespread growth and expansion, not to mention a series of record sales and profits along the way. By 2013, Sheetz had amassed more than 450 company-owned and -operated stores across six states, including Pennsylvania, Maryland, Virginia, West Virginia, Ohio, and North Carolina, along with more than 15,000 employees.

It was a far cry, indeed, from the early days of the Sheetz Dairy Store, with Bob, Aunt Bess, and John Mickel serving up Dubuque chipped ham with a French stick back on Fifth Avenue. In 1952, Bob's first-year sales netted $36,000—a tidy sum for a start-up convenience store with a young entrepreneur at the helm. In 1969, Sheetz surpassed $1 million in sales for the first time; just three decades later, in 1999, the company eclipsed $1 billion in sales. In 2012, the vaunted *Forbes* magazine ranked Sheetz as the No. 61 privately held company. That same year, the company accrued $6.4 billion in revenue. In recent years, Sheetz has enjoyed consistent rankings in terms of overall employee satisfaction, a benchmark that, as with Total Customer Focus, is particularly gratifying for Steve, who places premiums on employee retention and safety. In 2012, Sheetz ranked as the 16th best place to work in Pennsylvania—the company's 11th consecutive year to make the list—as well as the only convenience store to crack the commonwealth's top 100 places to work. In addition to ranking as Ohio's sixth best place to work, Sheetz ranked as the 21st best place to work in Virginia. In North Carolina's most recent survey of best places to work, Sheetz ranked third—the company's most impressive ranking in any state's listings.

As with the company's early days, when Bob—following his father Jerry's example—would give generously to the underprivileged, Sheetz continues to blaze new horizons in terms of charitable deeds. The company's For the Kidz program is but one example of the culture of giving that the Sheetz family supports. In 1992, district managers Dan McMahon and Charlie Campbell led the company's employee base in raising $12,000 to help out 126 disadvantaged children during the holidays. Since its humble beginnings in the early 1990s, the initiative has raised $11.6 million to support more than 69,000 children.

As much as the company celebrates long-standing programs such as For the Kidz, the management team also values the need for change to spur on additional innovation and to explore new retail frontiers. To this end, Stan succeeded Steve in 1995 as the company's president, with Steve assuming the role of chairman of the board. In 2013, Joe Jr. took over the reins, bringing in a new generation of leadership for the 61-year old company. Such transitions are in keeping with the company's philosophy. As Steve has famously remarked, "We are always working to create the business that will put Sheetz as we know it today out of business." Inherent in Steve's comment is the idea that Sheetz must inevitably move forward with new innovations so as to refuse to become stagnant, as it had during the early 1980s. But as Adam Sheetz (born December 24, 1982), director of regional operations, notes, "It's a little bit of an arrogant statement. I don't disagree with Steve, but what it essentially says is, 'We're going to be the company that puts Sheetz out of business.' It doesn't say, 'We're going to be the company that puts Exxon or 7-Eleven out of business.' It says that we are the standard in our industry, in the convenience-store industry. If we're going to get better, we have to put ourselves out of business because we're already better than the competition."

With each new innovation, the company remains in the vanguard of the convenience store industry. Today, these innovations are inextricably linked with the company's branding strategy, a concept that has evolved from a loose advertising scheme into a fully consolidated idea. As Mike Lorenz, executive vice president of petroleum supply, asks, "What is the Sheetz brand? It's hard to describe because everything that we do is our brand, from our stores, to our offer, to the way we treat our customers and employees. Everything is the embodiment of the brand, which is just so enormous, so big. Everything that we do is the brand." For this reason, the company takes every opportunity—no matter how obscure or unusual—to underscore its mission. As Mike notes, "Even today, some people still see us as a gas station. We ask, 'What's the first thing that comes to your mind when you think of Sheetz?' They often say 'gas.' We want them to say 'food.' Ultimately, we're trying to get them to recognize us as a restaurant that sells gas." As if to underscore this notion, Sheetz intern Jimmy Coonan points out that "the Sheetz brand will never truly be achieved because, by design, it's always changing. As long as they're working towards that carrot at the end of the stick, as long as they're charging forward, then they're going to progress and get better and become a better company, become more successful. But the brand is never really a finite thing because Sheetz, by design, is always about moving onto the next big thing."

Take the colorful Sheetz tanker and grocery trucks, for example, that patrol the company's six-state service area. They are key implements in the company's branding concept. As Mike Lorenz notes, the tankers are especially vital elements in maintaining the massive gas inventory required for several hundred Sheetz stores. But they are also, to quote Steve, "rolling billboards" that share in a branding effort across a multi-state region. Each year, Sheetz tanker trucks travel more than 16 million miles across the company's service area. For Steve, the tankers perform a signal role in reminding a growing customer base, once again, that they *can* eat at a convenience store that also sells gasoline—automotive products and freshly prepared food under the same roof. But to secure this goal, says Steve, the tanker trucks must be spick and span. "We've got to have clean, really clean tankers," says Steve, "because the most important thing in the food and beverage business when you talk to consumers is they want it to be clean where they buy their food. They want the people to be clean, facilities to be clean." To underscore the marketing connection between the tanker trucks and food service, says Steve, "we've got to make doubly sure these tankers are clean, which is not an easy task. They've done an amazing job, our drivers, keeping those tankers clean and they take great pride in driving a clean tanker. Obviously, we spend a lot of money washing trucks—but it's an important investment in our mission—and in our brand." As Buddy Casado, president of CLI Transport, the company's trucking subsidiary, remarks, "Spotless, clean trucks means spotless, clean restaurants."

While the Sheetz branding strategy plays a significant role in speaking to the company's customer base, so does its advertising strategy, which has become known—and sometimes with great controversy—for being edgy, says Louie, but always memorable. The company's marketing arm has been very shrewd over the years in employing the Sheetz name, with its terminal Z, to great effect. In order to increasingly market the company's retail food initiatives, Sheetz has designed colorful, envelope-pushing campaigns like its "Crispy Frickin' Chicken" program. As Steve recalls, "With 'Crispy Frickin' Chicken,' people were like, 'You can't say 'crispy frickin' chicken!' Once again, though, it allows us to open up new markets for people who don't even realize that Sheetz has food. Way back, when we started our soda fountain offer, we called them 'BFD' to stand out. People would ask me, 'What's a BFD?' And I would answer, slyly of course, 'It's a big fountain deal!'" As Stan observes, "With marketing, are you going to cross the line or not? The 'Frickin' Chicken' one, that was clearly on the line. We got phone calls from city councilmen saying, 'I'm going to pass a law to ban your billboards.' All kinds of threats like that." And then there was the infamous "Grab Lunch by the Meatballs!" campaign for a new sandwich line. As Steve's wife, Nancy, remembers, with campaigns like that "you can't please everyone but it's fun! Sometimes, you have to have a sense of humor." Ultimately, though, the edgy Sheetz marketing campaigns succeed precisely because they lodge themselves into the public consciousness, if sometimes a little bit irreverently.

With its tanker trucks, commercials, and billboards in full force, Sheetz has clearly poised itself to become, in Mike's words, a "restaurant that sells gas." With an increasing accent on Sheetz as a "convenience restaurant," Louie remarks, the company will continue to remake itself. "You might see us in different places: airports, campuses. We'll generally have fuel, but maybe not. Maybe you'll see our stand-alone food and beverage brand in a more pedestrian setting. Could that be in a mall? Could be. Could that be in an airport? Could be. Could be on a college campus, too. People are already saying, 'Why don't you put up a store in my building?' Those are innovations worthy of consideration, I think," says Louie. "Imagine this," he adds. "Imagine our food brand going mobile and bringing our food brands and menu offer directly to you, where you are. Where do people congregate? Public events, schools, campuses, large employers, office parks. What if we pushed the boundaries of convenience even further and brought our product line directly to you?"

In a conscious effort to push the Sheetz brand into new vistas of the American mind-set, the company has launched a variety of social media initiatives aimed particularly at the millennial culture—the late teens and twentysomethings who make up a key demographic, both for now and well into the future. "This age group is increasingly important as we define our food and beverage future," says Louie. Obviously, this demographic offers the highest potential for lifetime Sheetz business, while also innately buying into the concept that Sheetz offers a convenience restaurant and not merely a gas station. As Louie adds, "They're also more willing to try new things—new product innovations. And they don't just eat three standard meals a day. They eat around the clock!" As always, Louie adds, "the main goal is to connect with millennials and learn more about how they think so we can live up to their expectations, and in doing so, increase food and beverage sales. We want to shift consumers' perception of Sheetz as mainly a gas station with food to a stand-alone food establishment."

For this reason, the company has employed Ashley Sheetz, a recent Penn State University graduate in marketing from the Smeal College of Business, as its first social media coordinator. Millennial customers, says Ashley, interface with the company on a level that is increasingly governed by social media. "Millennials seem to be more active on Facebook than our other fans," Ashley remarks. "They send us more pics and videos, and they're more likely to retweet or follow us if their friends are." To this end, the Sheetz Facebook page has amassed more than one million fans. In order to connect with this growing and powerful segment of the company's customer base, Sheetz increasingly utilizes mobile technology—namely, customer-focused digital communications, which incorporate online food ordering, mobile apps for smart phones, new website designs, enhanced order-point development, and innovative thinking around digital menu boards. "Ultimately, social media expands our relationship with Sheetz fans and strengthens their brand loyalty," says Tammy Dunkley, Sheetz corporate advertising manager.

As Sheetz continues to assert itself as a "convenience restaurant," social media and advertising act as the vehicles through which the company will define itself. But as Sheetz has learned, time and time again, advertising and marketing are but two elements in the company's strategy for growth. As the Sheetz management team has discovered through years of hard-wrought experience, customer satisfaction requires a concrete effort—sometimes quite literally—to capture market share and ensure profit margin.

Sheetz enjoys a long history of charitable endeavors, most notably the For the Kidz initiative, which dates back to 1992, when district managers Dan McMahon and Charlie Campbell led the company's employee base in raising $12,000 to help out 126 disadvantaged children during the holidays. Since its humble beginnings, the initiative has raised $11.6 million to support more than 69,000 children. After his death in August 2006, Joe Sheetz's strength of character was celebrated through the establishment of the Big Joe Scholarship Fund, which affords the children and stepchildren of the company's employees with scholarship opportunities based upon their academic success, overall excellence of character, community involvement, and leadership.

Sheetz has also been a longtime supporter of the American Cancer Society.

Since 1978, Sheetz has held annual employee celebrations and recognition events at the Seven Springs resort in Pennsylvania. As part of the company's tradition, the Sheetz leadership team performs skits and dons costumes related to a particular theme. In the upper left photograph, Bob Sheetz poses as Uncle Sam. In the other three images, Steve Sheetz poses as a snake charmer (upper right), General Patton (lower left), and a frightened and caged jungle explorer.

At the company's 1990 Seven Springs event, the Sheetz leadership team participated in the Miss Sheetz Pageant. Counterclockwise from top left are Joe Sheetz, Louie Sheetz, Stan Sheetz, Charlie Sheetz, Phil Schreyer, Rick Vanevenhoven, and Steve Sheetz.

Phil Schreyer (left) leads the charge as the Sheetz team presents its 40th anniversary cake at the 1992 Seven Springs celebration.

Stan (left) and Steve Sheetz (right) in a "Red Hot" promotional poster for the company's annual Seven Springs celebration.

Sheetz has enjoyed regional—and sometimes national—attention for its advertising campaigns. The "Eating Is Believing" campaign was rolled out in support of the MTO phenomenon.

One of the company's most notorious advertising blitzes challenged customers to "Grab Lunch by the Meatballs."

While some customers found the "Crispy Frickin' Chicken" campaign to be offensive, others enjoyed the company's risqué sense of humor. The Frickin' Chicken campaign was eventually suspended when Sheetz learned that the advertisement violated a registered trademark held by the Fricker's restaurants of Miamisburg, Ohio.

As with such earlier campaigns as "Grab Lunch by the Meatballs" and "Crispy Frickin' Chicken," some customers found the depiction of the busty, alluring woman promoting Sheetz's "New Value Menu" to be in questionable taste.

The Sheetz campaign promoting "$4 Footlongs" came under fire after Subway Restaurants alleged that the Sheetz advertisements violated the spirit of its copyrighted "$5 Footlong" campaign and would be confusing to its customer base. In February 2009, a Virginia federal judge found in Sheetz's favor, arguing that Sheetz had sufficiently differentiated its advertisements in order to avoid any product confusion.

Family Matters is the company's long-running employee news magazine. The August 2010 issue celebrates the convenience store chain's growing "Passion for Food" as its product sector with the most growth potential.

The massive fleet of Sheetz trucks operates as a set of "rolling billboards," according to Steve Sheetz, that advertises the company's products, while also cementing the image of cleanliness that is essential to its Total Customer Focus program. This photograph was taken during an August 1998 Sheetz company picnic at Idlewild Park in Ligonier, Pennsylvania.

Operated by Sheetz subsidiary CLI Transport, Sheetz's fleet of trucks is a great source of pride for the company as well as being emblematic of the cleanliness that Sheetz hopes that its customers will associate with the company. As Buddy Casado, president of CLI Transport, observes, "Spotless, clean trucks means spotless, clean restaurants." In this photograph, the Sheetz Advisory Board poses alongside a company tanker truck advertising MTO sandwiches. Pictured are, from left to right, (first row) Bob Sheetz, Stan Sheetz, Chet Cadieux, Joe M. Sheetz, Gene Kephart, Steve Sheetz, Bob Hannan, Louie Sheetz, and Dan McMahon; (second row) Erez Goren, Jim Broadhurst, J.V.D. (Dyck) Fear, and Joe S. Sheetz.

CLI Transport's drivers undergo rigorous training, as demonstrated by the 1993 graduating class of CLI drivers. From left to right are (first row) John McConaughy, Fran Zajac, Jim Williams, Lennie Waters, Norm Goulding, and Ken Chesnutwood; (second row) Dave Zander, Clyde Trout, Bob Capes, Harry McHenry, Mike Mamula, and Tom Garizas.

The colorful, custom-painted Sheetz Hummer greets customers and employees across the region at new store openings, employee recognitions, and company special events. (Photograph by Roseanna Shumskas.)

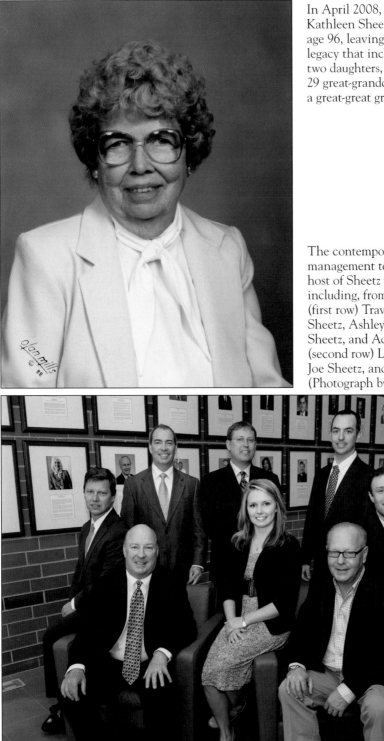

In April 2008, family matriarch Kathleen Sheetz passed away at age 96, leaving behind a family legacy that includes five sons, two daughters, 24 grandchildren, 29 great-grandchildren, and a great-great grandchild.

The contemporary Sheetz management team features a host of Sheetz family members, including, from left to right, (first row) Travis Sheetz, Steve Sheetz, Ashley Sheetz, Stan Sheetz, and Adam Sheetz; (second row) Louie Sheetz, Joe Sheetz, and Ryan Sheetz. (Photograph by Jamie Empfield.)

Twelve

SHWELLNESS, SUPER SHEETZ, AND OTHER RETAIL ADVENTURES

As the Sheetz executive team fully recognizes, freshly prepared food is clearly the future of Sheetz and the sales leader that it will ride into the years to come. As Travis points out, "We've realized that we have to advertise more than ever. Over the years, we've used gasoline to bring people to our site because gasoline is such a hook, but to use gasoline to get people to come and convince them you have good food is kind of counterintuitive. So we've changed the look of our buildings to be more reflective of restaurants. They're more red brick with awnings; they're just different looking. The simple truth is that you've got to build food business."

To meet this need, folks like Rick Cyman, vice president of design and construction, work to reshape the nature of Sheetz locations to become more adaptable to the needs of retail food customers. In order to signal that Sheetz stores are restaurants, new locations feature outdoor seating with umbrellas. To increase customer capacity, says Rick, "you naturally have to have bigger lots. Most convenience store operators were satisfied with 20 parking spaces; Sheetz wanted 35 and 40 spaces to make our locations more customer friendly." But to prepare and serve food, Rick adds, "things need to evolve. The kitchen size needs to change, as does the checkout counter. We wanted more cooler doors. We wanted seating areas and then, most recently, we wanted drive-thrus and rear entrances and vestibules, larger bathrooms and so on." Yet as Sheetz contemplates such changes in order to establish a foothold with its convenience restaurants, the company must inevitably refashion its older locations to fit the newer model. "They'll get renovated or rebuilt as quickly as we can," says Rick. "We're trying to renovate 30 a year. We often rebuild them from the ground up because, with a remodel, we can't quite make it look and act like a new store. There are certain dynamics in a new store that are difficult to achieve with a remodel." Such dynamics also include greater customer interest in car washes at Sheetz stores as well as drive-through service.

While the company works to remake the interior and exterior look of its locations, Sheetz also vows to redefine itself as a purveyor of freshly made food items. "What defines us now is the convenience restaurant," says Steve. "That is the best of the convenience store, while keeping the gas and core products. We will continue that with quality food and indoor and outdoor seating." With these goals in mind, Chef Dan endeavors to find new and innovative ways to signal fresh, homemade elements with the Sheetz food line. "We have to look for any way for us to increase the signs of freshness in our products," says Chef Dan, "whether it's the packaging, the product itself, how we execute it, how we prepare it. Any cue that I can get in the consumer's mind to increase the true freshness of the product is a victory," he adds. "And people want more flavor than ever before. Take the recent success of Chipotle; they're all about freshness and flavor. I was inspired to enhance our spices by their example. Spice is huge. People want a flavor adventure today." In 2001, the company's efforts to define itself as a restaurant were buoyed when Sheetz won a Silver Plate Award from the International Food Manufacturers Association. The convenience restaurant had once and truly arrived.

As Ryan Sheetz (born December 20, 1982), director of brand development, notes, the recent culinary successes of Chef Dan and others indicate that Sheetz has a new market niche on its hands, that it cannot rely forever on gasoline and cigarettes as enduring sales leaders. As his cousin Adam adds, "We've got to have whatever consumers want. Whatever fuel they want to fuel their vehicles with in the future—natural gas or electricity perhaps. As my father, Stan, would say, 'You've got to have your balance sheet in good enough shape to make that capital investment when it becomes clear what the winning technology is.' " As yet another attempt to fulfill customer desires, Sheetz has been involved in a long-standing effort to provide beer sales in its locations in Pennsylvania, where the state exerts tight control on the retail beer and liquor business. In many ways, Sheetz's interest in beer sales picks up where the company left off, years earlier, by stocking beer during the Sandwich Saloon era. As Bob notes, "Year after year, we go to the National Association of Convenience Stores meetings, where we interact with people from every state in the union. And we got to hear them talk about beer sales and how much profit was generated just in beer sales alone. But we're jealous! We're in Pennsylvania; we're not allowed to sell beer."

As Stan adds, "We surveyed our customers. 'Would you like to be able to buy beer in a Sheetz store?' We got a 70 percent positive response rate." But in the company's home state, says Stan, "it has become a spider web of laws and rules and regulations. In Pennsylvania, there are nine different licenses that you can use to sell beer, and that doesn't include the special permit licenses you can get for festivals and county fairs." After fighting their way through the legal morass, Sheetz was finally able to market beer sales at its flagship convenience restaurant on Seventeenth Street in Altoona—the "Super Sheetz," as it is known in local folklore. But to accomplish this, Sheetz had to establish artificial boundaries in order to meet the spirit—and the letter—of prevailing state laws. As Stan points out, "The law is you can't sell beer at the same establishment that you sell gasoline. That's the law in Pennsylvania. So we deeded the gasoline on a separate piece of property and, hence, you can only pay for gas at the gas pump. The Seventeenth Street location is the only store that we have that takes cash at the pump." Moreover, says Stan, "the law says we need a physical barrier between the gas pumps and the store. So we built a speed bump as our physical barrier, and the liquor control board finally gave their approval."

Such efforts are indicative of the company's dedication to providing their customers with every possible and desired aspect of their retail offer—no matter the cost. Sheetz's supreme gesture in this regard involves the most significant capital expense in the history of the company, the construction of the Sheetz Distribution Center in Claysburg, Pennsylvania. For Ray, it is a central "building block" in the future of Sheetz, as it demonstrates the company's most concerted attempt to provide its customers with freshly made, reliable products across the entirety of the convenience store chain. Built for more than $22 million, the massive Sheetz Distribution Center provided the company with 240,000 square feet. An additional 150,000 square feet would be constructed at a later date to accommodate growth, increasing the building's capacity to 390,000 square feet. Built adjacent to the distribution center, the company's bakery, ready-to-eat facility, and Sheetz Brothers Kitchen allow Sheetz to produce a variety of bakery and ready-to-eat items, including sandwiches, salads, and other convenience restaurant foods, that can be delivered fresh every day to company stores across the region. Remarkably, the Claysburg distribution center opened its doors for business on September 11, 2001. As the nation faced a looming national crisis with that morning's terrorist attacks, Sheetz assigned the distribution center's first two deliveries—truckloads of fresh water and beverages—for transport to the first responders in New York City and Washington, DC. A second distribution center is currently being constructed in Burlington, North Carolina, at a cost of $32.8 million. Expected to open in December 2014, the new, 245,000-square-foot distribution center will service the growing number of Sheetz locations in North Carolina and Virginia.

While projects like the company's distribution centers demonstrate its investment in providing its customers with fresh, high-quality products—key elements in the Total Customer Focus mission—Sheetz continues to seek out new ways of not only recruiting, but retaining its growing employee base. For this purpose, Sheetz recently constructed a wellness center adjacent to the Claysburg distribution center. Known as the Sheetz Shwellness Center, the facility includes a health and fitness center, an indoor track, and a variety of gym equipment. It also features educational implements, including a learning center with meeting rooms and video-conferencing capabilities. As Stan notes, "Sheetz has been voted by our employees as among the best places to work for more than a decade because we do everything we can to acknowledge their value and keep them happy in their jobs. The Shwellness Center is part of our culture of wellness, to give employees and their families the tools they need to achieve and maintain good health."

As initiatives such as the distribution center and wellness facility so clearly remind people, the convenience store industry has changed in countless ways in the more than six decades since Bob first opened the Sheetz Dairy Store for business. But the company's overarching strategy has remained decidedly unchanged. It is, and always will be, about bringing the highest-quality retail offer to customers and creating and maintaining in-store traffic. As Bob points out, "My driving goal was always to increase sales. If you came into my store, I would welcome you and talk your ear off; I wanted merchandise going out the door, so I gave you a free loaf of bread. 'Buy a half pound of chipped ham,' I would tell you, 'have a free loaf of French stick!' And then I gave you a free newspaper to boot. I just wanted activity. I wanted people coming into the store—and later coming back again and again for more." Bob's words, as meaningful today as they were back in 1952, are the heart and the essence of the story of Sheetz.

Since 2001, Sheetz has been consistently ranked as one of the best places to work in Pennsylvania. Sheetz has received similar honors across its six-state service area. (Photograph by Kenneth Womack.)

The most recent Sheetz logo (center), with its gleaming brick-red finish and its "Fresh Food Made to Order" motto, accents the company's effort to become known among its customer base and beyond as a "convenience restaurant." The Sheetz contemporary convenience store design (bottom), complete with customer-friendly outdoor seating, promotes each location's restaurant fare.

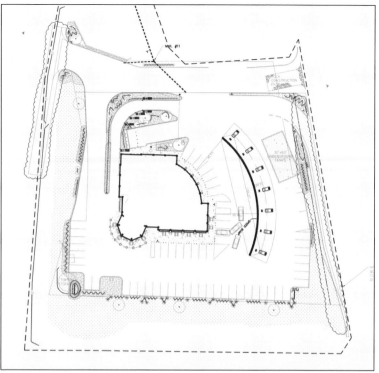

At right is the site plan for the company's flagship "convenience restaurant" on Seventeenth Street in Altoona, pictured below. Known locally as the "Super Sheetz," the location opened in 2004 and encompasses more than 10,000 square feet.

Pictured here are the exterior designs of a contemporary Sheetz "convenience restaurant" (above) and the new Sheetz location in Claysburg, Pennsylvania, near the company's distribution center (below). (Below, photograph by Chynna Herman.)

Rick Cyman is vice president of design and construction for Sheetz.

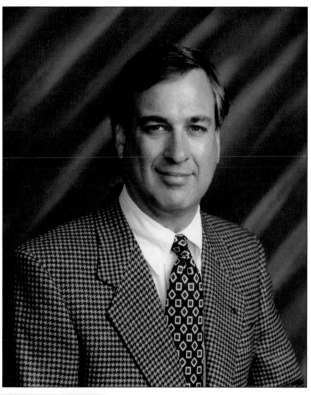

Mike Lorenz is the executive vice president of petroleum supply.

The mammoth Sheetz Distribution Center in Claysburg, Pennsylvania, opened in September 2001. Built at a cost of more than $22 million, the distribution center encompasses over 240,000 square feet. (Photograph by Kenneth Womack.)

Completed in 2001, the distribution center allows the company to provide its customers with freshly made, reliable products across the entirety of the convenience store chain. Built adjacent to the distribution center are the company's bakery, ready-to-eat facility, and Sheetz Brothers Kitchen. (Photograph by Kenneth Womack.)

This interior photograph from the Sheetz Brothers Kitchen shows where employees prepare bakery and ready-to-eat items for distribution to more than 450 Sheetz locations.

Adjacent to the distribution center in Claysburg, the Shwellness Center includes a health and fitness center, an indoor track, and a variety of gym equipment. It also features educational facilities, including a learning center with meeting rooms and video-conferencing capabilities. (Photograph by Kenneth Womack.)

At the November 2012 grand opening of the Shwellness Center are, from left to right, state representative Jerry Stern; Steve Sheetz; state senator John Eichelberger; Stan Sheetz; Bill Young, director of compensation and benefits; and Travis Eckels, manager of Marathon Health and the Shwellness Center's wellness programs.

In October 2013, Joe Sheetz assumed the role of chief executive officer for the company, holding the key leadership position previously filled by Bob Sheetz, Steve Sheetz, and Stan Sheetz.

ABOUT THE AUTHOR

Kenneth Womack is professor of English and integrative arts at Penn State University's Altoona College, where he also serves as senior associate dean for academic affairs. He is the author of three novels, *John Doe No. 2 and the Dreamland Motel* (2010), which earned *ForeWord Reviews'* Bronze Award for Literary Fiction; *The Restaurant at the End of the World* (2012), which won the Gold Medal for Regional Fiction in the Independent Publishers Book Awards, and *Playing the Angel* (2013). Womack is also the author or editor of numerous works of nonfiction, including *Long and Winding Roads: The Evolving Artistry of the Beatles* (2007) and *The Cambridge Companion to the Beatles* (2009), which was named as *The Independent's* "Music Book of the Year." He lives in Altoona, Pennsylvania, with his wife, Jeanine, and their family. (Photograph by Marissa Carney.)

Discover Thousands of Local History Books Featuring Millions of Vintage Images

Arcadia Publishing, the leading local history publisher in the United States, is committed to making history accessible and meaningful through publishing books that celebrate and preserve the heritage of America's people and places.

Find more books like this at
www.arcadiapublishing.com

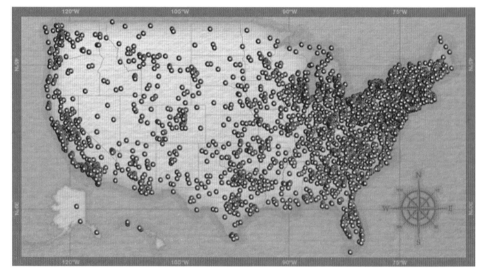

Search for your hometown history, your old stomping grounds, and even your favorite sports team.

Consistent with our mission to preserve history on a local level, this book was printed in South Carolina on American-made paper and manufactured entirely in the United States. Products carrying the accredited Forest Stewardship Council (FSC) label are printed on 100 percent FSC-certified paper.

MADE IN THE